JOHN C. FRÉMONT
AND THE REPUBLICAN PARTY

A Da Capo Press Reprint Series

THE AMERICAN SCENE
Comments and Commentators

General Editor: Wallace D. Farnham
University of Illinois

JOHN C. FRÉMONT
AND THE
REPUBLICAN PARTY

By Ruhl J. Bartlett

DA CAPO PRESS · NEW YORK · 1970

A Da Capo Press Reprint Edition

This Da Capo Press edition of
John C. Frémont and the Republican Party
is an unabridged republication of the
first edition published in Columbus, Ohio, in 1930

Library of Congress Catalog Card Number 73-87663
SBN 306-71763-8

Published by Da Capo Press
A Division of Plenum Publishing Corporation
227 West 17th Street, New York, N.Y. 10011

FRÉMONT AND THE
REPUBLICAN PARTY

JOHN C. FRÉMONT AND THE REPUBLICAN PARTY

By
RUHL JACOB BARTLETT
Tufts College, Mass.

THE OHIO STATE UNIVERSITY
COLUMBUS , , , , OHIO

Manufactured in the
United States of America

To
Lela May Bartlett

PREFACE

THE era of American history from 1850 to 1860 affords an unusually fertile field for the study of American politics. During that epoch the course of American development was changed; movements which had been gaining momentum for several decades were consummated, and new forces gained supremacy. It was a period of transition, of rapid political and economic alteration, and of profound social upheaval. Men were moved deeply by their thoughts or their emotions, and acted vigorously. It often happens that during such times of stress a leader appears who, under ordinary circumstances, would have remained obscure. Such a person was John C. Frémont.

The fact that Frémont had but little political training, only a meager amount of political experience, and no adequate claim to statesmanship, not only increases the interest in his rise to a place of prominence in the political and military history of the United States, but it is also an evidence in itself of the confusion that prevailed. His career provides an excellent connecting link between the political campaigns of 1856 and 1864, and furnishes, moreover, an example of the complicated political intrigue which was so characteristic of the middle period of the nineteenth century. The purpose of this study, therefore, is neither to investigate and interpret the underlying social and economic causes for the political phenomena of the times, nor to supply a complete biography. It aspires to present the political career of John C. Frémont in its proper setting, in the hope that it will shed a little additional light upon the confused politics of the period.

It would be impracticable for me to acknowledge all of the persons and institutions that, in one way or another, have contributed to the completion of this study. I am under deep obligation to Professor Arthur C. Cole of Western Reserve University, who first suggested this subject, and without whose aid, personal interest, and understanding, it would not have been completed. It is gratifying, also, to recognize the assistance and encouragement which I have received at various times from Professor Homer C. Hockett and Professor Carl Wittke of The Ohio State University, Professor Beverly W. Bond, Jr. of the University of Cincinnati, and from my colleague, Professor Halford L. Hoskins of Tufts College.

R. J. B.

WEST SOMERVILLE, MASS.
APRIL, 1930

CONTENTS

CHAPTER I

PATHFINDER AND SENATOR
1813 – 1850

JOHN C. FREMONT, explorer, soldier, and politician, has been one of the enigmas of American history. Many of his contemporaries ascribed to him a place of esteem which was occupied by no other American citizen.[1] He was thought of as the embodiment of the spirit of the American frontier, the true emancipator of the slaves, and both the explorer and conqueror of the Pacific slope.[2] Yet in the estimation of others he was a mere spoiled child of fortune, who possessed "all the qualities of genius except ability," and whose "activities were so near the line between great deeds and charlatanism that it was difficult to distinguish the pose from the performance."[3] Beyond doubt he held an extraordinary position in the popular imagination during the meridian years of the nineteenth century; volunteers swarmed to his standards during the Civil War, throngs gathered to hear him speak, and the mere use of his name was supposed to insure the success of a business enterprise.

The life of Frémont from the time of his birth at Savannah, Georgia, January 21, 1813, to his entrance into politics in 1850 was a series of very clearly marked episodes. He was successively a student at Charleston College, a teacher of mathematics, a surveyor and explorer, and a soldier in the Mexican War. His story is not without romance; it is notably one of adventure. He was capable of an elopement with the daughter of Senator Benton and of writing a report

---

[1] Hubbard to Jay Cooke, May 5, 1869; quoted in Oberholtzer, *Jay Cooke*, I, 103.
[2] Senator Nesmith of Oregon said: "He was given credit for finding everything west of the Rocky Mountains." Elridge, *Beginnings of San Francisco*, I, 374.
[3] Royce, "Frémont," *Atlantic Monthly*, LXVI (Oct., 1890), 548 ff.

of an exploring expedition which influenced Brigham Young to lead his Mormon flock to Utah. By 1850 he had become a notable figure, and his name was familiar to the majority of the American people. His emergence, however, into the arena of national politics could not be foreseen in 1850.[4]

While in California Frémont had authorized the purchase of a tract of land later known as the Mariposa estate. When his career in the army came to an abrupt close in 1848, he decided therefore, to make California his home.[5] Although it was his intention to develop his estate into a cattle ranch, after the discovery of gold he turned his attention to mining; but after a short time he perceived the political possibilities of his situation. It is patent that the gold rush produced a population in California almost by magic, and the local alcalde administration was not popular. Agitation therefore for the establishment of a new government led to the election of a constitutional convention.[6]

Frémont had taken very little if any part in the movement for the constitutional convention; in fact, he apparently had little interest in California politics until he decided to be a candidate for the United States senatorship. A considerable number of men had senatorial aspirations, the most prominent being Thomas Butler King, William M. Gwin, John W. Geary, Robert Semple, and H. W. Halleck. In this array of candidates Frémont was undoubtedly the most popular. He was widely known on account of his connections with the conquest of the state, and it was supposed that through his relationship with Senator Benton he would be better fitted than any other candidate to secure favorable legislation for California.[7] He declared that he was thoroughly a Democrat "by association, feeling, principle, and education," and that he adhered to the "great principles of

---

[4] Nevins, *Frémont, the West's Greatest Adventurer* (2 Vols., New York, 1928) is the best general biography of Frémont.

[5] The facts regarding his court-martial and his journey to California may be found in *Proceedings of the Court Martial of Colonel Frémont* (30th Cong., 1st Sess., Sen. Ex. Docs., No. 33); Benton, *Thirty Years View*, II, 716; Nevins, *op. cit.*, II, 368-87.

[6] Goodwin, *The Establishment of State Government in California*, p. 254.

[7] Bancroft, *History of California*, VI, 311.

the Democratic Party."[8] Finally he championed the already popular idea of a national railroad connecting California with the East. Frémont, therefore, was selected on the first ballot to represent California in the United States Senate.[9]

When the bill for the admission of California as a state was approved, and the Senators from California were admitted to the Senate, Senator Frémont announced that he would confine his labors in the Senate to the furtherance of measures essential to the welfare of California.[10] A few measures which later came into political discussion should be mentioned here.

On September 11, there was under consideration in the Senate a measure providing compensation for the African Colonization Society for expenses incurred while caring for seven hundred and fifty slaves who had been recaptured by an American ship from a slaver. When the vote was taken to engross this bill for the third reading, Frémont voted with the minority against the measure, and that minority was composed almost exclusively of Southern senators.[11] About the same time a measure was proposed abolishing the slave trade in the District of Columbia. Frémont voted against a substitute proposal of Senator Seward to abolish slavery in the District, but voted for the abolition of the slave trade.[12] A little later he again voted against a measure providing for abolition in the District.[13] It is to be noted, therefore, that while in the Senate Frémont allied himself neither with the abolitionists nor with the radical proslavery group. In minor matters of a non-partisan nature he was generally found on the side taken by Senator Benton. The only active part played in the Senate by Frémont was in regard to California affairs. He read the titles of eighteen bills which he intended to introduce into the Senate.[14] According to Bancroft these

---

[8] Public announcement of Fremont; quoted in Bigelow, *Life of Frémont*, p. 389.
[9] Goodwin, *op. cit.*, p. 261.
[10] 31st Cong., 1st Sess., *Globe*, p. 1791.
[11] 31st Cong., 1st Sess., *Senate Journal*, p. 623.
[12] *Ibid.*, p. 626 (Sept. 12, 1850).
[13] *Ibid.*, p. 647.
[14] 31st Cong., 1st Sess., *Globe*, p. 1793 (Sept. 10, 1850).

measures were drawn up by Senator Gwin,[15] but that idea is untenable in view of the fact that Senator Gwin opposed some of them and informed the Senate that he would introduce others as substitutes.[16] The only bill introduced by Frémont which occasioned debate to any extent during the time he was a member of the Senate was a measure providing for the settlement of land claims. The provisions of this bill which made the decision of a land commission final against the United States, and a decision in the District Court in favor of a claimant final against the United States, was opposed by Senator Ewing of Ohio, Senator Gwin, and others.[17] Frémont had little support other than that of Senator Benton, and the session ended before any of these measures proposed by Frémont were acted upon. The work of carrying out the plans for California legislation was done by Senator Gwin.

In accordance with the custom of the Senate when a new state is admitted into the Union, Senators Frémont and Gwin drew lots to determine their classification, Frémont drawing the short term which would expire March 4, 1851.[18] The first session of the Thirty-first Congress continued until within about eight weeks of the time for the opening of the second session; but Frémont, not waiting for the second session, hastened at the expiration of the first to California to work for his re-election to the Senate.[19]

In California Frémont made San José, the state capital, his headquarters and established a journal, the *San José Argus*, to work in his behalf.[20] There was a great amount of confusion in California over party lines. According to the *California Courier*, the state legislature was composed of twenty-nine Whigs, eighteen Democrats, and six unclassified members.[21] If the six unclassified members voted with the

---

[15] Bancroft, *op. cit.*, VI, 346.   [16] 31st Cong., 1st Sess., *Globe*, p. 1811.
[17] *Ibid.*, pp. 2045-47 (Sept. 27, 1850).
[18] 31st Cong., 1st Sess., *Senate Journal*, p. 617.
[19] Goodwin, *op. cit.*, p. 342.
[20] *New York Tribune*, June 19, 1856, quotes a letter from J. Winchester, Editor of the *Argus*, to the *Tribune*.
[21] Dec. 9, 1850.

Democrats, the Whigs would still have a majority of five, according to this classification. But the *Daily Pacific News*, which supported Frémont, declared that the Democrats had a majority in the legislature.[22]

The principal candidates for the Senate besides Frémont were Solomon Heydenfeldt, Thomas B. King, John Geary, John B. Weller, and James A. Collier. John B. Weller was a native of Ohio, a former Whig member of Congress from that state, and a member of the boundary commission appointed by President Polk after the Mexican War. Solomon Heydenfeldt was the leader of the so-called proslavery Democrats in California, and King and Geary had been candidates at the previous election. The election was influenced by the fact that one faction of the legislature wanted the state capital moved to Vallėjo, and they were willing to trade senatorship votes for this project. Thus mutual suspicion among the various factions delayed the vote on the senatorship.[23] When a vote was finally taken on February 15, 1851, Frémont was in the third place, with only eight votes, while twenty-five were necessary for a choice.[24] The balloting continued, Frémont rising to second place on the fifty-third ballot, but falling back to third place by the one hundred forty-second, when the legislature decided that further balloting was useless and deferred all further attempts at election until January 1, 1852.[25]

During the campaign strict party lines were more or less obscure, but Frémont and Heydenfeldt both were considered as Democrats.[26] The friends of each of these candidates threatened to vote for King; and, although the threats were not carried out, the failure of the two Democratic factions to unite prevented a Democratic selection.[27] When the legislature met again the following year Frémont did not contest the election.

[22] Feb. 13, 1851.   [23] *Daily Alta California*, Jan. 25, 1851.
[24] *Ibid.*, Feb. 20, 1851. King received fifteen and Heydenfeldt sixteen votes.
[25] *California Courier*, Mar. 1, 1851.
[26] *Ibid.*, Nov. 27, 1851. The Sacramento County Whig convention opposed Frémont because he was a Democrat.
[27] *Daily Alta California*, Feb. 24, 1851.

In the course of Frémont's later career this election was important in its relation to the slavery question. The editor of the *San José Argus* declared later that Frémont failed to receive the entire Democratic support because he was a "free state" man,[28] and Frémont wrote to Charles Robinson in 1856 that it was the slavery issue that defeated him in California.[29] Undoubtedly there were two groups in the Democratic party of that state, but neither Frémont nor Heydenfeldt made any specific declaration of his stand on the slavery question, and the journals of the day could not distinguish between them on that issue.[30] It is doubtful, therefore, that in 1856 Frémont's friends could show that their candidate was a martyr to the cause of freedom in 1851. Some of the Democrats who opposed Judge Heydenfeldt based their opposition on the charge that he had been a "disunionist" while in Alabama,[31] but no such charge could be lodged against Weller, on whom the Democrats could have united, had Frémont been willing.[32] Certainly the Whig opposition to Frémont was not based on any consideration of the slavery question,[33] and the evidence strongly indicates that the controversy within the party was one of personalities rather than one of principles.

With the conclusion of this episode, Frémont seems to have lost all interest in politics. He devoted his attention to various business enterprises, but chiefly to the development of his Mariposa estate. There he encountered many difficulties. The miners looked with great aversion upon large holdings, and Frémont had not established a clear title to his land. Moreover, he needed capital, which was most easily found in Europe. Thus, in 1852, Frémont and his wife set out for London and Paris.

---

[28] J. Winchester to *New York Tribune*, *New York Tribune*, June 19, 1856.

[29] *New York Tribune*, Apr. 10, 1856.

[30] *Daily Pacific News*, Mar. 18, 1851, declared it could not tell which candidate was favored by the proslavery party. It should be remembered that California had just adopted a constitution prohibiting slavery.

[31] San Francisco correspondent (Mar. 5, 1851), *New York Tribune*, Apr. 8, 1851.

[32] *Ibid.*

[33] Letters and communications to *New York Tribune* from California, Jan. 9 and 22, Feb. 12 and 20, and Mar. 8, 1851.

The pleasant sojourn in Europe was cut short by the news that the Government of the United States was about to undertake a series of five surveys to determine the most practicable route for a railroad to the Pacific. Since Frémont was the most famous of the Rocky Mountain explorers, it was thought that he would be chosen to lead one of the expeditions. He returned to Washington, but only to meet with disappointment in being omitted from the list of leaders.[34] No direct evidence has been found to indicate the exact time when Frémont ceased to consider himself a member of the Democratic party, but it may be that this event was the determining factor in his opposition to the Pierce administration. To be sure, his later conduct may be explained on the grounds that he, like Benton, opposed what each thought was extreme in the proslavery policy of the President, but the former situation will remain as an interesting clue to his actions.

Frémont's ardor for exploration, or his determination not to be cast aside, led him to prepare at private expense, and to undertake in 1854, a new exploratory expedition across the Rocky Mountains. The designated purpose of the undertaking was to demonstrate the practicability of constructing a railroad along the general route which Frémont had attempted to explore in 1848. This time the proper passes through the mountains were found, and the success of the expedition, which was completed during the winter season, was supposed to add further proof of the feasibility of that route. In 1855 Frémont returned to the East, both to further his business enterprises and to write an account of his expedition. He was thus engaged when he was caught in the whirlwind of national politics.

---

[34] Dellenbaugh, *Frémont and '49*, p. 432.

CHAPTER II

CANDIDATES AND CONVENTIONS
IN 1856

THE complicated state of American politics in 1856, which was largely responsible for the nomination for the presidency of such a man as John C. Frémont, defies easy definition. In few decades of American history has the drama of politics been more varied than in the period from 1850 to 1860. Old leaders passed from the stage, old political organizations either ceased to exist or survived with lessened prestige, and new men with new mottoes became the heroes of the hour. It was a period of uncertainty, of rapid change in public sentiment, and of feverish excitement among the masses. The people of that decade witnessed the collapse of the Whig party, the phenomenal effervescence of the Know-Nothing party, and the birth of the Republican party. The Whigs could not survive the defeat of 1852; but the new Republican party, based on moral sentiment and sectional jealousy, was obliged to fight for its existence against the combined opposition of the Democrats and Know-Nothings.

The enactment of the Kansas-Nebraska Act in 1854 was the general signal to various factions in the Northern states for a renewed and venomous attack upon the policy of the Democrats regarding slavery in the territories. Out-and-out Free-Soilers, Free-Soil Democrats, and many old-time Whigs hastened to join the fray, but there was a divergence of opinion as to the most effective strategy that might be used. If a new party was to be formed, it appeared that the name "Republican," adopted by many enthusiastic mass meetings in the summer of 1854, was most appropriate.

In the meantime, the Know-Nothing party was forging to the front. That organization was the result of a recrudescence of the anti-foreign sentiment which was occasioned by the great influx of foreigners during the late forties and early fifties. In the spring of 1850, Charles B. Allen organized the order of the "Star-Spangled Banner," which, together with a majority of the members of an older organization, the "United Americans," and various other similar organizations, became popularly known as the Know-Nothings.[1] During May and June of 1854, a "Grand Council" for the entire United States was organized, and the Know-Nothing party was ready to take its place among American political parties. There was a general political upheaval in 1854, which was strikingly illustrated by the congressional elections. According to the *Whig Almanac* the number of Democratic Congressmen was reduced from 157 members in the Thirty-third Congress to 36 members in the Thirty-fourth Congress. While this amounted to a party revolution, the opposition was a heterogeneous mixture of Whigs, Republicans, and Know-Nothings, which, as yet, was far from being a unity and therefore might divide some for and some against the Democrats on certain issues.

The Know-Nothings were reasonably elated over their success in 1854, and decided to hold a national meeting in June of the following year to adopt a set of party resolutions and to strengthen the party organization. When the Grand Council met at Philadelphia, June 5, 1855, it immediately found itself in a controversy over the admission of delegates from Alabama and Louisiana, where the Know-Nothing organizations admitted Catholics to membership.[2] In the discussion that arose out of this controversy, it was disclosed that the Southern delegates were more interested in the attitude of the Alabama and Louisiana delegates on the slavery question than in their religious views.[3] The Southern members who wished to avoid a slavery controversy were at odds with the majority of the Northern members, who

---

Desmond, *The Know-Nothing Party*, p. 50.

[2] *New York Tribune*, June 7, 1855.

[3] Speech of Neil Brown of Texas, quoted in *New York Tribune*, June 7, 1855. The Louisiana delegates were excluded by a vote of 44 to 77, the 44 votes being cast by Southern delegates.

issued an address to the people, declaring for the admission of Kansas as a free state.[4]

The dissension among the Know-Nothings was hailed by the Republicans as an indication that a comprehensive anti-slavery movement was imminent; but such was the state of political confusion that the election of 1855 did not offer much promise for the immediate success of the Republican party. The general trend, however, was in their favor; for it became more evident, as time went on, that the American issue could not stand against the sectional appeal.[5]

In such a situation the first Republican convention was held at Pittsburgh, February 22, 1856. It was a mass meeting rather than a convention, but it was well attended by men from the Northern states.[6] The only prominent member from a Southern state was Francis P. Blair, of Maryland. He had been a prominent Democrat, but when President Polk came into office in 1845 he ceased to be a leader of the party and supported Van Buren against Lewis Cass in 1848.[7] He mildly supported President Pierce, but was disgruntled over the failure of his son, Montgomery Blair, to receive the chief justiceship of the District of Columbia. He denounced the Kansas-Nebraska Bill, and came out in support of the Republican party in December of 1855.[8] Although he was mentioned as a Republican candidate for the presidency, it was supposed that he favored Thomas H. Benton for that office.[9] He was made the president of the Pittsburgh convention,[10] and became one of the most prominent supporters of Frémont for the presidency.

The convention was a gathering of enthusiastic anti-Nebraska men but the speeches were studious attempts to avoid any issue that would cause disunion among the various

---

[4] *New York Tribune*, June 15, 1855.
[5] Letters of Greeley to Dana, published in the *New York Sun*, May 19, 1889, throw much light on this contest. See also *New York Tribune*, Dec. 5, 1855.
[6] *Cleveland Herald*, Feb. 18, 1856; *National Intelligencer*, Feb. 25, 1856.
[7] McClure, *Recollections*, p. 44.
[8] *New York Tribune*, Dec. 19, 1855.
[9] The *Age* (Augusta, Me.), Jan. 24, 1856; *Pittsburgh Post*, Mar. 16, 1856; *Washington Evening Star*, Feb. 27, 1856.
[10] *National Intelligencer*, Feb. 25, 1856.

elements represented. A set of resolutions was adopted which embraced the three points upon which a union could be made; non-extension of slavery into the territories of the United States, admission into the Union of Kansas as a free state, and general opposition to the political influence of the South. The task before the new organization was to discover a candidate who could preserve the unity maintained thus far. There was no dearth of aspirants for the presidency, and the reasons for the failure of the various prominent candidates in the race for the nomination, were, to a great extent, the reasons for the selection of John C. Frémont.

In 1854, a group of men, among whom Gideon Welles and Senator Preston King were prominent, attempted to initiate a movement in favor of Sam Houston of Texas.[11] For a time the *Chicago Tribune* was favorable to this idea,[12] and it appeared that Houston might gain a respectable amount of anti-Nebraska support.[13] In February of 1855, however, he delivered a speech at Boston in which he defended the Southern point of view on the slavery question, and pointed out that the South had not originated the Kansas-Nebraska Bill and that the prosperity of the North was occasioned by the influx of cheap foreign labor and not by its freedom from the slave system.[14] This open stand on the sectional issue deprived him of whatever anti-Nebraska following he may have had,[15] although there was some scattered support for the Texas hero as late as March, 1856.[16]

In the Republican nominating convention of 1856, John McLean, of Ohio, had a following larger than that of any other candidate except Frémont. A good many considerations seemed to indicate him as an available candidate for the Republican party in 1856. He had been identified with the antislavery faction in the North as early as 1848, when he was considered by the Free-Soil party as a possible candidate

---

[11] John Williams to Gideon Welles, Oct. 17, 1854. Welles MSS.
[12] *Chicago Tribune*, Feb. 21, 1855.
[13] *Liberator*, Mar. 20, 1855.
[14] *Chicago Tribune*, Mar. 1, 1855.
[15] *Ibid.*; also *Liberator*, Mar. 20, 1855.
[16] Washington correspondent, *New York Tribune*, Mar. 21, 1856.

for the presidency. Later he was associated with the Whigs, but declared that he hailed with "unmeasured satisfaction" the rise of the Know-Nothing party.[17] On the other hand, he was the most conservative candidate in the Republican canvass of 1856. He did not favor the election of Chase to the governorship of Ohio because he felt that Chase was ultra in his views on the slavery question,[18] and he did not approve, so he said, of those politicians who seemed to think that statesmanship consisted in arraying one party of the Union against the other. He further believed that the territories should be open to all the people of the Union, the question of slavery being settled when the territory became a state. McLean's followers, therefore, believed that the Whigs, Know-Nothings, and conservative antislavery men, as well as those who opposed slavery agitation, should be united on the basis of his candidacy.[19] But McLean did not understand the temper of the new Republican party. His refusal to assume an aggressive anti-Nebraska position enabled Charles A. Dana to speak of him as an "old fogy," and a "marrowless old lawyer" who should be brushed aside.[20] When Israel Washburn was inclined to favor him, Horace Greeley could point out that "all of the old earnest anti-slavery men" did not like him.[21]

Among the conspicuous Republican leaders of 1856, none was more anxious to receive the presidential nomination than Salmon P. Chase of Ohio. His political experience consisted of one term in the United States Senate and the governorship of Ohio after the expiration of that term. Originally a Democrat, he became an ardent antislavery enthusiast and took up with the Republican movement. His success in the Ohio governorship race in 1855, in uniting the Know-Nothings and antislavery Democrats with the Repub-

---

[17] McLean to Robert Parish, Mar. 3, 1855. McLean MSS.
[18] McLean to John Teasdale, November 2, 1855; quoted in Salter, *Letters of John McLean to John Teasdale*, p. 137.
[19] Thomas Ford to McLean, November 27, 1855. McLean MSS.
[20] Dana to Pike, May 21, 1856; quoted in Pike, *First Blows of the Civil War*, p. 338.
[21] Greeley to Washburn, June 13, 1856. Israel Washburn MSS.

licans, led him to believe that he could accomplish the same feat in the presidential race.[22] Influential friends had already directed his mind toward that goal, but the fact is that Chase was without any considerable following among the influential political leaders of his party. Governor Grimes of Iowa, and Charles A. Dana of New York[23] might be listed among his followers, but in general he had little support outside of the Free-Soil Democrats.[24]

If the mantle of the Republican presidential nomination had fallen to the most worthy member of the party, it undoubtedly would have descended upon William H. Seward of New York. He had been an uncompromising opponent of Democracy for thirty-odd years and was looked upon as "the incarnation of Northern hostility to the South on the ever waging question of slavery."[25] His re-election to the Senate in 1855 was widely acclaimed by the antislavery press, and in June of that year the *New York Times* declared that there was no other person in the United States of sufficient prominence to be named as a popular candidate for the presidency.[26] Less than a year later, however, the same journal was convinced that he should not be considered as a candidate.[27] This change in opinion was due to his recognized and well-known antipathy toward the Know-Nothings.

As a New York politician, Seward had courted the good will of the foreign population, advocating, when Governor of the state, special schools for the children of the foreign-born, conducted in their language and instructed by teachers of their own religious faith.[28] When the Know-Nothing movement developed he assumed a strong stand in opposition, letting it be known that he would have nothing to do with any move on the part of the Republicans that involved a compromise with that element.[29] As a natural result, the

---

[22] Chase to Bingham, October 19, 1856. Chase MSS (Pa. Hist. Soc.).
[23] See Von Holst, *Constitutional and Political History*, VII, 366.
[24] Smith, *Political History of Slavery*, I, 226.
[25] The *Albion* (N. Y.). February 10, 1855.
[26] June 28, 1855.   [27] April 22, 1856.
[28] *Seward's Works*, II, 215.
[29] "Seward's Speech at Albany," *Seward's Works*, IV, 225.

Know-Nothings were bitterly hostile to him.[30] Many of the prominent men of the Republican party believed that the Know-Nothings should not be opposed and denounced as Seward had denounced them, but should be conciliated.[31] Stating it another way; many Republicans were anti-Nebraska Know-Nothings.[32] In the words of Governor Grimes of Iowa, there was "too much asperity of feeling" against Seward throughout the country to permit his selection.[33] The situation called for a man who would be acceptable to all the various factions, an available man; and Seward could not qualify.[34]

This summary of the political status of the various Republican candidates and the reasons for their rejection explains why it was possible for a man unknown to the party councils to become the party leader. That such a situation might develop was clearly foreseen by various politicians; and, contemporary with its development, a small group of adroit political leaders selected a man and skillfully presented his qualifications. How it came about that Frémont was the man selected, and how his candidacy was so successfully conducted furnishes an interesting episode in the history of American politics.

Frémont had taken no active part in politics since his defeat in the senatorial race in California. Yet he had not been lost entirely to the public eye. His last exploring expedition presented him again to the public notice; and that fact, together with his known hostility to President Pierce, attracted to him the attention of Nathaniel P. Banks and Henry Wilson of Massachusetts,[35] who with Francis P. Blair of Maryland began to consider him as a possible candi-

---

[30] A. B. Views to Weed, November 28, 1855. Weed MSS. Weed, who was probably Seward's most trusted political adviser, was assured by Views that the Know-Nothings entertained a deep prejudice against Seward.

[31] Chase is an example.

[32] The *Cincinnati Gazette* displays a good example of this sentiment.

[33] Grimes to Chase, April 8, 1855; quoted in Salter, *Life of Grimes*, p. 68.

[34] J. H. Rice to Fessenden, May 15, 1856. Fessenden MSS.

[35] According to George C. Bates of California, Banks and Wilson were first attracted to Frémont when they heard that he had refused to be a Democratic candidate. See speech of Bates printed in the *Ohio State Journal*, September 1, 1856.

date for the presidency.[36] In furtherance of this idea a
meeting of a select group of politicians was arranged and
held at the home of Morton McMichael of Philadelphia,
editor of the *North American*, and the qualifications of Frémont were discussed.[37] The exact date of this meeting is not
known, but it was held some time during the summer of
1855, and the evidence seems to show that other meetings
were held and that the general impression was that Frémont
would be a good candidate.[38]

Blair began to make arrangements for the organization
of the Republican party on a national basis and therefore
invited Chase, Bailey, Sumner, Banks, Seward, and Preston
King to visit him at Silver Spring. At that meeting, which
was held in December, 1855, he presented the name of
Frémont and let it be known that he favored him as a presidential candidate.[39] By that time the movement for Frémont
was gaining considerable momentum. Gideon Welles was
writing about it in December,[40] and the *Baltimore Sun* knew
of Frémont meetings that were held in Baltimore.[41]

Early in 1856, N. P. Banks visited John Bigelow of the
New York Evening Post in order to solicit his aid in the
movement for Frémont.[42] Banks urged that the Republican
party would make no headway unless a leader was found
who was not connected with any of the old parties, and who

---

[36] The editor of the *Daily Pennsylvanian* (Phila.) said that he knew that Blair
was the original inventor of the movement for Frémont. *Daily Pennsylvanian*, August 23, 1856.

[37] G. Bailey to Chase, April 18, 1856. Chase MSS (Pa. Hist. Soc.). Bailey was
the editor of the *National Era* (Washington, D. C.), and although he did not support
Frémont he seems to have had accurate knowledge and his story is reasonable in view
of other known facts. There is a possibility, of course, that this may not have been
the first Frémont meeting; Senator Benton said that he had known about the movement for Frémont and had opposed it six months before most people knew anything
about it. Benton to Thomas Price; quoted in *Savannah Republican*, August 22, 1856.
Also during the summer of 1855, several journals mentioned that new and politically
inexperienced men were being considered. *North American*, June 25, 1855; *New York
Evening Post*, July 17, 1855.   [38] *Ibid.*

[39] Seward to Weed, Dec. 21, 1855; Seward, *Seward at Washington*, II, 264.

[40] Welles to (————), December 28, 1856. Welles MSS.

[41] *Baltimore Sun*, June 20, 1856.

[42] Bigelow, in *Retrospections*, I, 141, indicated that he knew of the Frémont
movement in 1856, but it is likely that he was interested in it before that. Bailey in
his letter to Chase (See footnote 37) said Bigelow was connected with it from the

possessed some quality that would attract popular attention. Bigelow was favorably impressed with the Frémont idea and invited several prominent men of New York to his home to discuss the matter.[43] Among them were Samuel Tilden and Edwin D. Morgan, the latter being favorably disposed toward the candidacy of Frémont.[44] Bigelow then began the composition of a biography of Frémont, which very soon began to appear in the *Evening Post*. Mrs. Frémont aided in its preparation and actually wrote the first few chapters.[45] The rapidity with which the movement for Frémont developed is well illustrated by the case of Schuyler Colfax of Indiana. In January he wrote to his paper, the *St. Joseph Valley Register*, stating that it looked to him as if only a miracle could unite the North; but by March, two months later, he was convinced that the miracle was being accomplished by Frémont.[46] Senator Trumbull was asked if Frémont did not possess traits of character and if he were not connected with some acts which would cause greater popular support than could be rallied for the "dignified and unromantic Governor of Ohio."[47]

Until about the first of April, the Frémont leaders made no attempt to launch a campaign to gain popular support for their candidate. So far the movement had been confined to something like a reconnaissance among the politicians of the party, but the time had come for an extension of the field of endeavor. On the last day of March the *Cleveland Herald* came out boldly for the nomination of Frémont,[48] and four days later Seward wrote that the majority of the Republican leaders at Washington were convinced that it would be expedient to make him their candidate.[49]

About the middle of April the appeal for popular support was launched in the form of a letter written by Frémont

beginning, and it is certain that the *New York Evening Post* mentioned Frémont's candidacy prior to Mr. Bank's visit. *New York Evening Post,* January 28, 1856.

[43] *Ibid.*   [44] *Ibid.*

[45] Jessie Frémont to Bigelow, July 7, 1856. Bigelow MSS.

[46] Hollister, *Life of Colfax,* p. 94.

[47] J. Bryant to Trumbull, Mar. 24, 1856. Trumbull MSS. Bryant had favored Chase.

[48] This was one of the earliest journalistic declarations for Frémont.

[49] Seward to Weed, April 4, 1856. Seward, *Seward at Washington,* II, 269.

to Charles Robinson, the leader of the Free-State party in Kansas.[50] Robinson had been a member of the California Legislature when Frémont was a candidate for the senatorship, and had written Frémont in regard to his nomination for the presidency. In answer to this letter Frémont intimated that he had been defeated in California on account of his antislavery ideas. He then complimented Robinson on his struggle to make Kansas a free state, and added, "I can only say that I sympathize cordially with you, and that as you stood by me firmly and generously when we were defeated by the nullifiers in California, I have every disposition to stand by you in your battle with them in Kansas."[51] Thus, at once, Frémont assumed the position of a political martyr to the so-called slave power and associated himself definitely with the anti-Nebraska faction. The letter received 'wide publication, and there was often favorable editorial comment, even in journals whose editors had expressed no preference for any candidate.[52]

By the time for the meeting of the Republican convention it is probable that among the party leaders there was no serious doubt that Frémont would be the nominee. Five days before the meeting, the New Hampshire Republican delegates were instructed to vote for him, and the central Republican committee of New York passed resolutions in his favor.[53] When McLean's manager and spokesman reached New York on his way to the convention, he was willing to concede the defeat of his candidate, who was the mainstay of the Frémont opposition.[54]

When the delegates began to arrive at Philadelphia two days before the opening of the convention, there was a final attempt to rally support for McLean. At a last-minute caucus of the Pennsylvania delegation, Neville B. Craig of Pittsburgh attempted to secure unanimity for McLean and

---

[50] This was a definite plan. See Congdon, *Reminiscences of a Journalist*, p. 152.
[51] *New York Tribune*, April 10, 1856.
[52] In every one of about 100 anti-Nebraska journals which were examined, it appeared in full or in part.
[53] *Baltimore Sun*, June 12, 1856.
[54] R. P. Spaulding to McLean, June 14, 1856. McLean MSS.

succeeded in gaining the support of all except two districts. Aside from the Pennsylvania delegation he had the support of a good portion of the Illinois delegates, a few from Maine, and probably a majority of those from New Jersey and Indiana.[55]

The Pennsylvania delegation and McLean's friends in general thought that Frémont should be satisfied with the vice-presidency.[56] This was not a new idea, and Frémont had instructed his representative at the convention, F. P. Blair, what to do in case the suggestion was made. "You may withdraw my name," he said, "as [you] may judge expedient, taking always the ground that I am a soldier in the ranks, and while I would feel honored, as every good soldier should, in being promoted, I am sincerely determined to apply time and energy in laboring for the common cause, should the convention determine to submit its leadership to other hands. But, while I shall in this event, [engage] myself actively to secure the great end, I am not able to give my time to the vice-presidency. Pray, therefore, do not let my name go before the convention in this connection."[57]

McLean's representative, Spaulding of Ohio, having sensed the trend of the convention, withdrew the name of his candidate, and Mitchell of Ohio did the same for Chase. Apparently, however, Spaulding had acted without consulting the Ohio delegation, and when after a short recess the convention reassembled, McLean was reinstated as a candidate.[58] As far as Chase was concerned, the movement for him collapsed without benefit of clergy, his erstwhile friends later explaining that the Frémont following was too strong to be successfully assailed, and that after a consultation it was decided to surrender with as much grace as possible.[59]

---

[55] *New York Tribune*, June 17, 1856; Konkle, *Life of Williams*, I, 296; *Pittsburgh Post*, June 16, 1856.

[56] *New York Tribune*, June 17, 1856, special correspondent.

[57] Frémont to Blair, June 17, 1856. Bigelow MSS.

[58] John Allison to McLean, June 20, 1856. McLean MSS.

[59] Hiram Barney to Chase, June 21, 1856. Chase MSS (Pa. Hist. Soc.). Barney said that Chase might have been more seriously considered if the Ohio delegation had been solidly back of him.

The choice of the convention for the vice-presidency fell to W. L. Dayton, an old Whig, and a prominent politician of New Jersey.[60] The selection of Dayton apparently was an attempt to please friends of McLean, for it was his following that urged him as a candidate. Some of the Pennsylvania delegates supported David Wilmot for a time, and the Know-Nothing element desired the selection of W. F. Johnson of Pennsylvania, who was already the Know-Nothing candidate for the vice-presidency. Thaddeus Stevens, however, refused to countenance the nomination of Johnson, on the score that it would injure the Republican cause in his state;[61] and Horace Greeley became alarmed, fearing that Johnson's nomination would endanger the chances of securing the German vote.[62] William B. Archer, an Illinois Congressman, rallied a hundred and ten votes for Abraham Lincoln, but Dayton was finally nominated without any very great difficulty.

The platform adopted by the convention did not take high ground on the antislavery question. It contained a specific denunciation of the policy of the Pierce administration in regard to Kansas, and a resolution that Kansas should be admitted as a free state into the Union. Nothing was said about the repeal of the Missouri Compromise; only a general statement was made that Congress should use its sovereign power over the territories to prohibit slavery and polygamy in them. Neither the Fugitive Slave Act nor the question of slavery in the District of Columbia was mentioned. Nothing was said concerning tariff or financial questions. A gesture was made to conciliate the Know-Nothings by a resolution declaring opposition to legislation which impaired the equality of rights among citizens; and a bid for the support of the Far West was made by a declaration favoring the construction of a railroad to the Pacific, with the aid of the Central Government.[63]

---

[60] *Ohio State Journal*, June 20, 1856.   [61] *New York Tribune*, June 21, 1856.
[62] Seward to family, July 7, 1856; quoted in Seward, *Seward at Washington*, II, 283.
[63] The platform is quoted in Johnson, *Three National Conventions*, pp. 43 ff.

Frémont was formally notified of his nomination on July 8, and his speech of acceptance is one of the most important documents of the campaign. Not only was it Frémont's only formal pronouncement during that period, but it was a forecast of the type of argument that the Republican leaders subsequently followed.[64] With varying phraseology the substance of this speech was repeated hundreds of times during the following months. Frémont began by saying that he had been placed in the van of a great movement to bring the government of the United States back to the principles of Washington and Jefferson; then, having alluded to that part of the platform which denounced the Ostend Manifesto, he entered upon the main consideration of his address— hostility to the South and opposition to the extension of slavery. On the first of these questions his thesis may be divided into four declarations: (1) the design of the United States in the establishment of independence was to prevent slavery extension; (2) a small slave-owning group in the South controlled the nation; (3) the main effort of this group was directed toward the defeat of the principles of the Revolution and the extension of slavery across the continent; (4) the strife in Kansas was the result of the policies of the South. In regard to the extension of slavery, he declared that the Kansas-Nebraska Bill was a scheme to deprive free labor of the areas reserved for it by a "solemn covenant," that Kansas was the only area of middle latitude in the West where free laborers could settle, and that these laborers look to constitutional rights to prevent slave owners from acquiring a monopoly of the soil which would force free laborers to work on the same footing as slaves.[65]

Frémont evidently felt that it was necessary to condemn the South for the extension of slavery and to show that its extension was inimical to the welfare of the North. If his

---

[64] The speech was printed in the majority of the journals of the time, i. e., *New York Tribune*, July 9; *Ohio State Journal*, July 12, 1856; also quoted in Hall, *Republican Party*, pp. 465-69.

[65] This is, of course, an analysis of Frémont's speech; the whole speech is worth reading.

declaration as to the purpose of the Republican party was indefinite, and if his statements in regard to historical events and their interpretation were made without due regard for the facts, nevertheless, his address sounded the keynote for the Republican campaign of 1856.

Assuming, as the facts seem to indicate, that there was a reasonable amount of unanimity within the Republican party in support of Frémont, his election would depend, to a great extent, upon the action of the Know-Nothing party. If it could retain its national organization, and assume in the North an anti-Nebraska character, as it did in Massachusetts in 1855, then the anti-Nebraska North would be divided, and Frémont's chance to succeed would be reduced. But if the Know-Nothings in the North would co-operate with the Republicans, as in Ohio in 1855, and at the same time contest the South on the American issue, then the outcome might be favorable for Frémont. The developments, therefore, within the Know-Nothing party were of prime importance to all parties in the campaign of 1856, and the trend of those developments was fairly well indicated by the time of Frémont's nomination.

When the national convention of the Know-Nothing party assembled at Philadelphia, the slavery issue came to the front immediately. The Northern members would not be conciliatory. They would either have their way or withdraw, and withdraw they did. The delegates that remained nominated Millard Fillmore for the presidency and Andrew J. Donelson of Tennessee for the vice-presidency. The anti-Nebraska Know-Nothings, now popularly called the "North Americans," met at New York, June 12, to select a presidential candidate. The *Baltimore American,* a Fillmore paper, believed that the majority of the delegates favored Frémont, whose nomination by the Republicans was already foreseen;[66] but there were groups who supported George Law, former Governor Ford of Ohio, Judge McLean, Nathaniel P. Banks, and Commodore Stockton of New Jersey.

---

[66] June 12, 1856.

Before the balloting began, a communication was received from the Republican executive committee, urging that there should be a union of all the anti-Nebraska forces, regardless of differences of opinion on other issues.[67] The committee to which this communication was referred recommended co-operation with the Republicans, but suggested that the convention should indicate by ballot whom it preferred for presidential and vice-presidential candidates, and then appoint a committee to confer with the candidates chosen and with the Republican convention. It was also recommended that the convention should remain in session until that committee of conference could make a report.[68] This convention then proceeded with the balloting which resulted in the nomination of Nathaniel P. Banks, and W. F. Johnson of Pennsylvania. It had been clear from the third day of the convention that the leaders were planning to annex this anti-Nebraska wing of the Know-Nothings to the Republican party. The nomination of Banks as a presidential candidate was tantamount to the nomination of Frémont, for Banks was one of the enthusiastic Frémont men.

When the Republican convention met on June 17, the resolutions of the "North Americans" expressing a desire for co-operation, were taken up for consideration. There was immediate objection to any formal co-operation, Joshua Giddings of Ohio, Seward, and Greeley being the leading opponents; and the matter was dismissed as far as the Republican convention was concerned. E. D. Morgan, the chairman of the Republican executive committee, was determined not to forego the "North American" support for Frémont, and in consequence their representatives were promised that if their convention would nominate Frémont, the Republicans would, in turn, induce their vice-presidential candidate, Dayton, to withdraw in favor of the "North American" candidate, Johnson.[69]

---

[67] *New York Tribune*, June 14, 1856.
[68] *New York Tribune*, June 16, 1856.
[69] Seward to family, June 26, 1856 and July 7, 1856; quoted in Seward, *Seward at Washington*, II, 279-83.

The "North American" convention, when it reassembled on June 19 to consider the report of its committee of conference with the Republicans, displayed considerable dissatisfaction over the failure of the Republicans to adopt a policy of open co-operation, and there was talk of making a declaration in support of Fillmore, rather than Frémont. The Frémont element obtained the upper hand, however, and the convention withdrew the name of Banks from the presidential race, but retained their candidate Johnson.[70] A few days later their executive committee wrote to Morgan reminding him of their agreement, and asking him to fulfill his promise by securing the withdrawal of Banks.[71]

Morgan was apparently but little concerned about the matter after he had secured the nomination of Frémont by the "North Americans," and, although he wrote to Dayton, he believed that the rising popularity of Frémont would overshadow the difficulty.[72] Discontent among the "North Americans" continued; and Israel Washburn, fearing that its continuance might be inimical to the interests of Frémont, took the matter up with Dayton independently. The latter, declaring that he had not been consulted when the agreement was made, and that in fact he had known nothing of the matter until July 11, refused to give any countenance to it whatever.[73] There the affair rested, until in August the "North Americans" decided to allow the whole controversy to be dropped.[74]

The Democratic party had, in the meantime, held its national convention.[75] The platform resolutions contained two noteworthy provisions; a direct denunciation of the Know-Nothings, and a specific indorsement of the Kansas-Nebraska Act as the best means for the settlement of the slavery question.[76] There had been no lack of aspirants for

---

[70] *New York Tribune*, June 20, 1856.

[71] A copy of this letter, dated June 30, 1856, was found in the Gideon Welles MSS.

[72] E. D. Morgan to Welles, July 9, 1856. Welles MSS.

[73] Dayton to Washburn, July 12, 1856. Washburn MSS.

[74] E. D. Morgan to Welles, August 8, 1856. Welles MSS.

[75] It met at Cincinnati, Ohio, June 2, 1856.   [76] *Daily Union*, July 6, 1856.

the presidential nomination. Among those most prominently
mentioned were President Pierce, James Buchanan of Pennsylvania, Henry A. Wise of Virginia, and Stephen A. Douglas of Illinois.[77]   In general the strength of Pierce was in
the lower South and in New England, while Douglas was
popular in the West, and Buchanan in the Middle States.[78]
Since the Republicans were planning to make the Kansas-
Nebraska Bill, and particularly the policy of the Pierce
administration in regard to Kansas, the main point of issue
in the campaign, they would have been glad if Pierce had
been selected as the candidate.[79]   But the cards were pretty
well stacked for Buchanan's nomination.[80]   He was from the
North, not immediately connected with the Kansas issue, and
he was popular in the important state of Pennsylvania.

In nominating Buchanan the Democrats did the expedient thing, for Buchanan, like Frémont, was the available
candidate for his party.   At the North he could be presented
as a solid, conservative statesman, while at the South his
acceptance of the party platform would secure support.   One
Republican declared that the Democrats had been as "wise as
serpents if not as harmless as doves."[81]   Seward noted that
Republican leaders in Washington were greatly concerned
over the prospects of success with Buchanan as an opponent,[82]
and it was reported that he would be hard to beat in Illinois.[83]

---

[77] *Cincinnati Enquirer*, November 27, 1855.

[78] This is shown by the votes in the convention. The Northwest would have supported Lewis Cass of Michigan if there had been any chance of his selection. *Detroit
Free Press*, April 24, 1856.

[79] Colfax to his paper; Hollister, *Colfax*, p. 140.

[80] John Slidell of Louisiana and Henry A. Wise managed the Buchanan forces in
the convention. See Tyler, *Letters and Times of the Tylers*, II, 521.

[81] A. C. Pennington to McLean, June 7, 1856. McLean MSS.

[82] Seward to family, June 10, 1856; extract in Seward, *Seward at Washington*,
II, 277.

[83] George Brown to Trumbull, June 3, 1856. Trumbull MSS.

CHAPTER III

LEADING ISSUES

The Democrats of 1856 were prone to emphasize the personal qualifications of their candidate—his long training in public office, and the conservative nature of his ideas. The Republicans could not make such an appeal; Frémont's nomination was not obtained by a demonstrated personal fitness for the presidency, but by his availability as a candidate. To be sure, certain enthusiasm was aroused for him on the basis of romantic episodes in his career and heroic qualities in his character, but his party was forced to present him to the people as representing certain party issues. The reasons, therefore, for his large following, as well as for his ultimate defeat, must be sought in the history of the campaign.

Among the outstanding characteristics of the Republican party of 1856, none was more striking or more dominant than its avowed antipathy toward the South, its customs, its industry, its manner of life, and its whole economic and social philosophy. An illustration of this is the Brooks-Sumner controversy, which offered an opportunity for the party spokesmen to make their position clear.

Senator Sumner of Massachusetts, called by Edward Everett a "wrong-headed" speculator,[1] was foremost among those who had convinced themselves that the Kansas-Nebraska Bill was a scheme for the extension of slavery. It was his desire to have the election center about the Kansas question; and he urged, therefore, that the immediate admission of Kansas as a free state should be advocated in order to bring the issue to the front.[2] Following up this idea he delivered in the Senate, speaking on two consecutive

---

[1] Edward Everett to Mrs. Charles Eames, July 5, 1855. Everett MSS.
[2] Weiss, *Life of Theodore Parker*, II, 178.

days, a remarkable invective called the "Crime-Against-Kansas" speech, which in reality was little more than a tirade against the South.[3]

This speech, on account of its denunciation of South Carolina as a state, as well as the scathing remarks about Senator Butler, led to the well-known attack on Sumner by Preston Brooks of South Carolina.[4] The attack furnished the opportunity for the continuation of the denunciation of the South. The influential editor of the *Springfield Republican*, Samuel Bowles, declared that the attack on Sumner and the action of Southern men in Kansas, showed "how impudent slavery had become" and demonstrated that it was necessary for the North to unite, not only to maintain "their equal rights but their independent existence as freemen."[5] While one journalist saw in the affair a further indication of the spirit of violence that obtained among the proslavery party,[6] another believed that the assault was really directed against the national system of government, and that it "was the most dastardly and most atrocious" ever so committed.[7] Whittier wrote in praise of Sumner's speech;[8] Henry Ward Beecher used the attack as a text for a sermon, in which Brooks appeared as a villain and a typical Southerner;[9] and the Republicans in general fanned the spark of indignation into a blaze, realizing the important political capital that could be made out of it.[10]

Frémont was the one who profited by whatever enthusiasm this affair aroused against the Democrats. It was a favorite expedient to have Sumner write a letter to be read to large Republican meetings, reminding people that he was still disabled, too ill even to return to his home.[11] It is impossible, of course, to determine the actual effect that this affair and the general hostility to the South exerted upon

---

[3] 34th Cong., 1st Sess., *Globe*, pp. 524-49.   [4] *New York Tribune*, May 21, 1856.
[5] Quoted in *New York Tribune*, May 24, 1856.
[6] *New York Evening Post*, May 24, 1856.
[7] *New York Tribune*, May 25, 1856.   [8] Pickard, *Life of Whittier*, p. 381.
[9] *National Anti-Slavery Standard*, May 21, 1856.
[10] McGuire, *Democratic Party in New York*, I, 321.
[11] *Sumner's Works*, VI, 11, 13, 15, 20, 22.

the election.   McClure in his *Recollections*, declared that
"it caused many scores of thousands of Democrats of natural
antislavery proclivities to sever their connections with the
Democratic party and unite in support of Frémont."[12]   If
elections are influenced by emotional appeals, then the oratory that was expended in describing the assault on Sumner
and the declarations concerning the barbarism of the South
must have been of considerable importance.

The growing sectional character of the Republican party
made it inevitable that the question of disunion would be a
prominent issue in the campaign.   The Democratic candidate, Buchanan, declared that all incidental issues were of
little importance in comparison with the "grand and appall-
ing issue of union or disunion."   "Should Frémont be
elected," he said, "he must receive one hundred and forty-
nine Northern electoral votes at least, and the outlawry proclaimed by the Black Republican convention at Philadelphia
against fifteen Southern states will be ratified by the people
of the North."[13]   Howell Cobb declared that in case of
Frémont's election he would go immediately to Georgia and
take the stump for secession.[14]   Robert Tyler believed that
the country was in great danger, but that the South would
be united and ready.[15]   John Tyler likewise believed that the
success of Frémont would be the end of the Union.[16]   Robert
Toombs said that the Union would end with the success of
Frémont, and that it should, for he believed that the object
of Frémont's friends was the conquest of the South.[17]

The disturbing question of secession shook the North as
well as the South.   Manufacturers, merchants, and bankers,
to some extent at least, were concerned over the question.[18]
The *Daily Pennsylvanian* said, "There is no disguising the
fact . . . that the great question of union or disunion has
been precipitated upon us by the mad fanatics of the North
and that it is a direct and inevitable issue in the presidential

---

[12] McClure, *Recollections*, p. 394.   [13] Moore, *Works of Buchanan*, X, 88.
[14] Dubose, *Life of Yancey*, p. 333.   [15] Tyler, *Times of the Tylers*, II, 531.
[16] *Ibid.*, p. 532.   [17] *New York Tribune*, August 18, 1856.
[18] Wilson, *Rise and Fall of the Slave Power*, II, 522.

contest."[19] The *Philadelphia Daily News* and the *Pittsburgh Post* stressed the same idea.[20] Buchanan wrote to Toombs that he could not understand why the people of Pennsylvania and Maryland could think of voting for Frémont, because those states would be border states in case of civil war and would suffer most.[21]

It seems that the cry of disunion was made more of in Pennsylvania than in any other Northern state, but it was not lacking elsewhere. Dickinson emphasized the sectional issue in Indiana.[22] Senator Trumbull received communications from Illinois, even before the nominating conventions had met, to the effect that the belief was quite general there that the Union was in great danger. [23] But as a general thing the Northern Democratic press did not advocate disunion in case of the election of Frémont. It deplored the sectional conflict occasioned by the rise of a sectional party and noted that disunion would be a possible consequence if such a party gained power.[24] The Southern press, on the other hand, was inclined to say that it would not be inevitable. The influential Frémont journals of the North belittled the secessionist scare. They said that such talk was merely for political effect, that it was an old trick of the South, and that since both the Buchanan and Fillmore papers were talking of disunion, Frémont was the only Union candidate.[25] At any rate, when the election was over, the *Cleveland Herald* believed that the fear of disunion had been potent enough in the North to cause the defeat of Frémont.[26]

Among the many characteristics of the campaign, the attempt on the part of both parties to secure the support of the German voters is not the least important. The Republicans appealed to the Germans on the theory that the strug-

---

[19] July 16, 1856.   [20] July 21, 1856.

[21] Phillips, *Toombs, Stephens, Cobb Correspondence*, p. 374.

[22] *Dickinson's Speeches*, I, 225 ff.

[23] J. Gillispie to Trumbull, May 29, 1856. Trumbull MSS.

[24] *Detroit Free Press*, July 26, August 2, 9, 1856.

[25] *New York Tribune*, September 22, 1856; *New York Herald*, August 21, 26, 1856.

[26] November 5, 1856.

gle for Frémont was really an effort to secure free and accessible land for immigrants. "Those Germans," declared the *New York Tribune*, "who wish to see a vast portion of the great West given over to slavery, thus shutting it out from themselves and their children . . . can do much toward it by helping to elect Buchanan. If, on the other hand, the Republican party shall succeed in electing Frémont and Dayton, there will be no more slave states; Kansas will be admitted with a free constitution, and that vast region will be open to the sons and daughters of freedom."[27]

Gustave Sturve appealed to his German followers with the statement that the South was attempting to make the free men of the North subservient to it as slaves. He declared that the Germans loved freedom, but should Buchanan be elected, the freedom of speech, press, assembly, and election would be destroyed.[28] A German paper in Cleveland declared that the immigrant was safe in the hands of the Republicans.[29] Without doubt, the idea that the existence of slavery degraded labor and that new slave territory tended to limit opportunity for poor immigrants who could not purchase slaves, had considerable appeal to the German population. But the Republicans did not appeal by ideas alone. Money was distributed to important German leaders,[30] some attempt was made to purchase Democratic German papers, and large German meetings were organized.[31] One of unusual size was held at New York in October. The speaker, Frederick Hecker, emphasized the undesirable conditions of white labor in the South. He said he could hear the whistle of locomotives carrying free men to free territory and could see the Goddess of Liberty "rise triumphant with her banner emblazoned with Frémont and freedom."[32] Similar meetings were held at Cincinnati and other German centers.[33]

---

[27] July 26, 1856.
[28] *New York Times*, July 25, 1856.
[29] *Wachter am Erie*, quoted in *Cleveland Herald*, June 27, 1856.
[30] Niles to Trumbull, Belleville, Illinois, July 15, 1856. Trumbull MSS.
[31] Villard, *Memoirs*, I, 59.
[32] *New York Tribune*, October 8, 1856.
[33] *Ohio State Journal*, June 21, also August 25, 1856.

The Republicans, however, were somewhat at a disadvantage in appealing for German votes; the Germans were traditionally Democrats, and the Republicans had united with the "North Americans," while the Democrats openly denounced the Know-Nothing party. The Democrats lost no opportunity to make the most of their advantage.[34]

There is no accurate way to determine how the German population voted in the election. The *Daily Globe* (Washington) stated that there were 60,000 German Turners who would vote for Frémont,[35] but the Turner society of Washington said that there were only 8,000 Turners in the United States. Koerner believed that the most of the Protestant Germans voted for Frémont.[36]

Among the influences in the election that did not appear to be very important, but existed none the less, was that of the tariff. James G. Blaine believed that, "disassociated from the question of protection, opposition to the extension of slavery was a weak issue in Pennsylvania."[37] Although none of the party platforms contained a tariff plank, the position of the Democrats could not have been misunderstood; there was no hope of protectionist measures under their rule. President Pierce, in his third annual message, declared that "it is now so generally conceded that the purpose of revenue alone can justify the imposition of duties on imports that in readjusting the important tables and schedules which unquestionably require essential modifications, a departure from the principles of the present tariff is not anticipated."[38]

The Republicans, on the other hand, were in a difficult position in regard to the tariff question. The desire to gain Democratic votes did not permit the insertion of a tariff plank in their platform, while the protectionists might well wonder what the policy of the administration would be if Frémont were in the White House. The merchants and

---

[34] Many Democratic pamphlets were translated into German.
[35] July 15, 1856.   [36] Koerner, *Memoirs*, II, 21.
[37] Blaine, *Twenty Years of Congress*, p. 196.
[38] Richardson, *Messages and Papers of the Presidents*, V, 388.

manufacturers were confronted with the danger of Southern secession and consequent curtailment of their markets if Frémont should be elected, while the Republicans did not hold out any definite promise of a protective tariff as a compensation.

Whatever amount of emphasis should be placed on the other various issues of the campaign, and whatever importance should be ascribed to the characteristics of the political situation, the Kansas-Nebraska Bill and the controversies in Kansas following its enactment furnished the subject matter for as much campaign oratory and as much campaign literature as all other subjects put together.[39] This was a natural consequence of the situation; the Republican party had arisen out of the Kansas issue in 1854,[40] and presumably the party would have been embarrassed for lack of an issue had Kansas come into the Union as a free state in 1855. By 1856, however, the party leaders realized how tremendously important the Kansas question was as a party issue.[41]

In March, 1856, the House of Representatives appointed

---

[39] Approximately four-fifths of the campaign documents issued by the Republican Association at Washington were on the Kansas question. See Celphane, *Republican Campaign Documents* (Washington, D. C.). An examination of the files of the *New York Tribune* will show that scarcely an issue failed to contain a great deal in regard to Kansas; and that was true of other papers. In a speech delivered at Faneuil Hall, Boston, Mass., Robert C. Winthrop, a Whig, analyzed the Republican campaign appeal as follows: "We all know by heart the recipe for a regular Free-Soil speech in these days. One-third part Missouri Compromise repeal, without one grain of allowance for the indisputable fact that it was proposed and supported by Northern men, and could not have been carried without their aid; one-third Kansas outrages by Border Ruffians, without one scruple of doubt as to the wisdom of Northern measures which, reasonable or unreasonable, have furnished so much of the pretext and provocation; one-third disjointed facts and misapplied figures, and a great swelling of words of vanity, to prove that the South is, upon the whole, the very poorest, meanest, least productive, and most miserable part of creation, and therefore ought to be continually teased and taunted and reproached and reviled, by everybody who feels himself better off. This, Mr. Chairman, is the brief prescription for a mixture which, seasoned to the taste and administered foaming, is as certain to draw and as sure to produce the desired inflammation as a plaster of Burgundy pitch or Spanish flies is to raise a blister." Quoted in Winthrop, *Memoirs of Robert C. Winthrop*, p. 188.

[40] For an exceptionally clear insight into the consequences that would accompany the creation of a sectional party, see R. B. Hayes to his Uncle, June 5, 1854; quoted in Williams, *Hayes*, I, 105.

[41] Horace Greeley realized its importance. See Greeley to Dana, January 8, 1856; quoted in *New York Sun*, May 19, 1899. Sumner's famous speech of May 19, 20 in the Senate was for the purpose of making it the issue.

a committee to investigate the Kansas situation in general and particularly the elections of 1855.[42] The majority of the committee, of course, was Republican; and its appointment was a counter stroke against the policy of the administration in regard to Kansas.[43] Affairs in Kansas, however, were effervescent, and before the committee could report on old disturbances new ones arose. The shooting of a sheriff by the Free-Soil faction was used as an excuse for the sacking of Lawrence by the proslavery party on May 21, 1856.[44] Three days later John Brown perpetrated the Pottawatomie massacre.[45]

In Congress, the Democratic leaders, realizing the potency of the Kansas appeal, began to plan definite measures to solve the controversy. On June 30, Senator Douglas introduced a bill into the Senate which embodied the essential features of a measure that had been proposed by Senator Toombs.[46] The measure provided that the President, with the advice and consent of the Senate, should appoint five commissioners, who, with the aid of the Secretary of the Interior, should make a list of all the legal voters resident in each county in Kansas. The legal voters were the male citizens, twenty-one years of age or over, who were bona fide residents on July 4, 1856, or residents three months before the election. The commissioners should then make an apportionment of members for a convention, make rules for regulating an election, and appoint election judges. The names of voters, the apportionment of convention members, the rules of election, and the names of the judges, all should be posted and made known to everyone. Finally, an election was to be held in November, and the convention chosen could, if it so desired, draw up a constitution. The President was authorized to use the military force of the nation under

---

[42] 34th Cong., 1st Sess., *Globe*, p. 1791 (Mar. 19, 1856).
[43] President Pierce had issued a proclamation which in effect sided with the proslavery party in Kansas. See, Richardson, *Messages and Papers of the Presidents*, IV, 285.
[44] See evidence submitted by *Report of Investigating Committee*.
[45] *Ibid.*, p. 1177.
[46] 34th Cong., 1st Sess., *Globe*, p. 1506.

the existing laws in order to execute the act, if called to do so by the commissioners.[47]

This measure, known as the Toombs Bill, was debated at considerable length. While Senator Hale complimented Toombs on the "sense of justice" that he had shown in drawing up the bill, and declared that he thought it was "almost unexceptionable," he found fault with some of its unimportant details.[48] Senator Collamer, a Republican member of the committee on territories, found no fault with the face of the measure, but objected to it because its purpose was to carry out the provisions of the Kansas-Nebraska Act.[49] He rather inconsistently favored the admission of Kansas under the Topeka constitution.[50] Senator Wade of Ohio made the outstanding attack on the measure. "The free-state men of Kansas," he said, "have done no wrong. Their only crime is that they loved freedom more than slavery."[51] It was enough for him to know that the President was to be given power to appoint the commissioners, for, he continued, "no man who has the least regard for the rights or dignity of the free states at heart, will consent to put liberty under the guardianship of our present President. It would be to make Kansas a slave state without a struggle, and to give to robbers, plunderers, and conquerors of Kansas the full benefit of the war they have so unjustly waged against the rights of freedom."[52] Senator Seward may have voiced the opinion of the majority of the Republican Senators when he said that he opposed the measure because it gave to the people of Kansas the right to choose between freedom or slavery, and he did not think they should have the right to choose slavery.[53] When the measure came up for decision on July 18, it passed the Senate by a vote of thirty-three to eighteen.

The Democratic press made the obvious comment that it was now up to the House to pass the Toombs Bill if peace

---

[47] Printed in *Detroit Free Press*, July 9, 1856.
[48] 34th Cong., 1st Sess., *Globe*, p. 1519 (July 1, 1856); also p. 1520.
[49] *Ibid.*, p. 1568 (July 8, 1856).
[50] *Ibid.*, p. 1570.
[51] Appendix to Congressional *Globe*, 34th Cong., 1st Sess., p. 754 (July 2, 1856).
[52] *Ibid.*, p. 757.   [53] *Ibid.*, pp. 762, 789, 796.

in Kansas were really desired.[54]   The *Detroit Free Press*
(Democratic), taking high ground on the matter, denounced
the proslavery territorial legislature, but pointed out that it
was a clear issue as to whether Kansas should come into the
Union under a constitution framed by the bona fide citizens
acting under the provisions of the Toombs Bill, or whether
the illegal Topeka government should be sustained.[55]   The
House, however, had no intention of passing the Toombs
Bill; it was not even considered.   They debated and passed
an act of their own, the Dunn Bill,[56] which was not the same
as the Toombs Bill,[57] and finally voted to admit Kansas
under its Topeka constitution.[58]

Douglas declared at the time, and believed later, that
the Republicans did not desire to restore peace to Kansas
until after the campaign was over,[59] and the Democratic
press announced the same view.[60]   As early as April, 1856,
Seward had notified Thurlow Weed that arrangements were
on foot to settle the Kansas struggle, which, he said, would
mean that the presidential issue would be lost; and he therefore urged Weed to organize meetings and get petitions
signed, and encourage the press to oppose the move.[61]   Eight
days after the passage of the Toombs Bill, Greeley urged
Schuyler Colfax to do what he could to adjourn Congress
before they got "entangled in some horrible and ruinous
compromise and destroyed."[62]   T. S. King lamented to Israel
Washburn that Congress was not adjourned, ". . . Douglas'
sly and slippery bill defeated and everything smoothed for
Frémont's election."[63]   Trumbull was informed that if the
House bill for the admission of Kansas were rejected by the
Senate, and the Toombs Bill defeated by the House, and

---

[54] *Daily Pennsylvanian,* July 16, 1856.   [55] July 17, 1856, July 29, 1856.
[56] 34th Cong., 1st Sess., *Globe,* pp. 1815, 1816, 1817.
[57] *Ibid.,* p. 1817.   [58] *Ibid.*
[59] Appendix to Congressional *Globe,* 34th Cong., 1st Sess., p. 844 (July 9, 1856);
Cutts, *Constitutional and Party Questions,* p. 108.
[60] *Philadelphia Daily News,* July 17, 1856.
[61] Seward to Weed, April 4, 1856; Seward, *Seward at Washington,* II, 269.
[62] He wrote again August 27 to urge the same thing; quoted in Hollister, *Life
of Colfax,* p. 100.
[63] July 17, 1856. Israel Washburn MSS.

then Congress should adjourn, the Republicans would have good political capital out of the Kansas situation.[64]

However that may have been, the Republicans were under the necessity of defending their action in regard to the Toombs Bill; that was not an easy task. The position that Seward had taken in the Senate,[65] which was substantially the same as that assumed by Greeley in the *Tribune*,[66] was that the people of a territory did not have the right to determine the slavery issue. The difficulty with their stand was that the Toombs Bill was not a popular sovereignty act, but an enabling act to permit the people of Kansas Territory to form a constitution. To deny the theory upon which this bill was set up was to deny the fact that the Government of the United States was one of equal states. The Republicans were further embarrassed by the fact that the Kansas investigating committee had reported that a fair election in Kansas could not be had without a new census, a well-guarded election law, impartial election judges, and the presence of United States troops at every voting place.[67] This was substantially what the Toombs Bill would have provided for.

In the meantime the Democrats were not idle in regard to Kansas matters. Buchanan promised to inaugurate a new system, and to deal with affairs in Kansas justly.[68] President Pierce appointed a new governor for Kansas, who, arriving at his post September 12, immediately ordered all bodies of armed men to disperse, and promised protection to the Free-Soil settlers.[69] By October the Democratic press could point out that the Missourians had been driven out of Kansas, the disorderly elements disarmed, and peaceful citizens adequately protected.[70]

The Republicans ardently attempted to retain the Kansas question as a political issue. The *New York Tribune* declared that a great deal of "buncombe" was being circulated

[64] M. W. Delaney to Trumbull, July 23, 1856. Trumbull MSS.
[65] 34th Cong., 1st Sess., *Globe*, p. 796.   [66] *New York Tribune*, July 12, 1856.
[67] 34th Cong., 1st Sess., *House Report 200*, p. 1767.
[68] *New York Tribune*, September 3, 1856.
[69] *Ibid*, September 17, 18, 1856.   [70] *Pittsburgh Post*, October 9, 1856.

about Kansas and affirmed that, although Governor Geary might prevent outrages on the part of the border ruffians, he would not do anything to make Kansas a free state.[71]   It was stated by one journal that the Governor used the troops of the United States to do what was formerly done by the Missourians,[72] and by another that he enlisted the Missourians in his service under the guise of state militia.[73]   About a month before the election, Henry Ward Beecher gave an address in New York during the delivery of which he exhibited a heavy chain with two large padlocks which he said had been placed around the legs of two free-state men in Kansas who had been forced to walk until the chain cut through their flesh.[74]   On the eve of the election an appeal was made to the voters of the North to vote for Frémont and thus prevent Buchanan and the South from forcing the slave system, not only upon Kansas, but upon the free states as well.[75]

[71] September 23, 1856.
[72] *Western Reserve Chronicle*, October 8, 1856.
[73] *Detroit Free Press*, quoted in *Western Reserve Chronicle*, October 15, 1856.
[74] *Ashtabula Sentinel*, September 25, 1856.
[75] *Ibid.*, October 23, 1856.   The assertion was that Buchanan would make Kansas a slave state and that as a result the South would be encouraged to demand that slavery be permitted everywhere.

CHAPTER IV

THE CAMPAIGN—WEST AND SOUTH

The Republican leaders entertained great hopes of carrying California for their candidate; Frémont was connected with the early history of the state and he was the champion of the idea of a railway to the Pacific, in which California was greatly interested. Events demonstrated, however, that the Republican party did not have smooth sailing in Frémont's state. A state convention meeting on April 30 adopted resolutions favoring the prohibition of slavery in the territories of the United States, the speedy settlement of land titles in California, unrestricted immigration, and free grants of land to settlers as well as free mining.[1] But the state nominating convention, calling itself the convention of the "People's Party," was not organized until October, and then conflict over local nominations was so intense that some of the delegates left the convention.[2]

Chase was informed in regard to California that, although a "Frémont party sprung up as if by magic," the leaders of it "were never known to have any sympathy with freedom or free soil," and some of them in their first speeches "took great pains to convince the people that no taint of such sentiments was attached to them."[3] It was stated that the Frémont men were interested only in the railroad schemes and California interests, and that the men who were employed to stump the state for Frémont were not of the recognized Free-Soil type.

Among the most prominent Frémont leaders were C. P. Huntington, Mark Hopkins, Leland Stanford, and Charles

[1] *Democratic State Journal* (Sacramento), May 1, 1856.
[2] *Daily Alta California*, October 10, 12, 1856.
[3] J. H. Purdy to Chase, November 5, 1856. Chase MSS. Purdy was writing from San Francisco.

Croker, all of whom were chiefly interested in the Republican party on account of their railroad interests.[4]   The campaign organ was the *Daily and Weekly Sacramento Times*, edited by Cornelius Cole, and the most important campaign speaker was Edward D. Baker.   Baker had been driven out of San Francisco because he opposed the vigilance committee, but when his success as a Frémont orator became known he was induced by the Republican members of that organization to return.[5]

The Know-Nothing state convention met at Sacramento on September 1.   The convention declared that since the Republican party was sectional, and therefore could not be successful, the only means by which California could secure a railroad to the East was by the election of Fillmore.   On all other matters the convention was hopelessly divided, and no general platform resolutions could be agreed upon.   The vigilance committee and the Kansas question were mentioned as issues, but without formal declaration, and some of the delegates advocated the support of the Democrats.[6]

The Democratic meeting, also in September, stole Frémont's thunder, and in resolutions urged the Federal Government to use its utmost and united exertion for the construction of a railway to the Pacific coast, and also urged the enactment of a liberal homestead law.[7]   In order that the Californians might have no doubt as to his railroad policies, Buchanan wrote to the Democratic state committee and defined his position.   He declared that Congress should appropriate money for the construction of a railroad, and that it had power to do so under the power to declare war, a railroad to the Pacific being a national defense.[8]

Thus the three parties stood essentially in the same position in regard to the main issue in California.   The Fillmore party, while pretending to make a stand for their candidate

---

[4] Cole, *Memoirs*, p. 112.
[5] Kennedy, *The Contest for California*, p. 127; Foote, *The War of the Rebellion*, p. 216.
[6] *Democratic State Journal*, September 4, 5, 1856.
[7] *Ibid.*, September 13, 1856.
[8] Moore, *Buchanan's Works*, X, 93.

and declaring that they could carry the state,[9] really began to disintegrate, and some of their journals joined the Buchanan ranks.[10] The Republicans, in spite of competition, continued to make the railroad issue the main point in their appeal for Frémont.[11]

This issue, however, was not the most potent in the mining districts of the state. The majority of the miners in California held to the doctrine of "free mines," which was a theory that the miner who first staked out a claim had thereby established an exclusive right to use the area designated for a mine. It so happened that on the eve of the campaign Frémont's title to his extensive Mariposa estate was confirmed by the Supreme Court and the miners were driven from the estate by force.[12] They regarded the establishment of that title as the first innovation against their rights, and therefore did not support the election of Frémont.[13]

Another factor in the campaign was the relation of Frémont with the firm of Palmer, Cook, and Company. Frémont had close business relations with that company, which, in the summer of 1856, was in disrepute in California on account of an illegal breach of faith in handling some securities belonging to the state. The affair did not attract much attention outside of the state, but within California it furnished the main point of attack against Frémont, and was used with vigor by several journals—especially the *San Francisco Morning Globe*.[14]

---

[9] C. D. Semple to Crittenden, August 12, 1856. Crittenden MSS. Semple declared that Fillmore would carry the state by 10,000.

[10] This was true of the *Mayesville Herald* and the *Sacramento Union*, quoted in *Democratic State Journal*, August 27, 1856. The newspapers of California did not hesitate to speak in plain language about an opposition journal. Note the following: "That ponderous old literary bloat—that vile old mercenary tool, that wretched time serving huckster and newspaper strumpet, has the impudence to speak of the *State Journal* as a paper which in the estimation of all respectable men has sunk so low that it is only read as a literary curiosity," etc., *Democratic State Journal*, July 31, 1856.

[11] *Daily Alta California*; quoted in *New York Times*, August 10, 1856. See also *Democratic State Journal*, August 9, 1856.

[12] Howard, *Reminiscences*, p. 87.

[13] *Weekly Ledger*, June 7, 1856.

[14] Elridge, *California*, III, 497.

Finally the two German newspapers of California opposed Frémont.[15] Thus the opposition of the miners, the German hostility, the Palmer, Cook, and Company affair, and the factional troubles within the party,[16] together with the fact that the Democrats took such high ground on the railroad issue, seem to explain the cause for Frémont's defeat in his adopted state.

In Iowa, as in California, the local situation was of great importance. The state had been Democratic, but in 1854, J. W. Grimes, on a Whig ticket, had won the governorship by a majority of over two thousand votes.[17] The Whig party of that year favored certain popular amendments of the state constitution, and championed a homestead law, internal improvements, and a temperance law.[18] The important fact was that the Democrats were divided; some favored the Kansas-Nebraska Bill, some the restoration of the old Missouri Compromise line, and some desired to pass over those issues entirely and to take a direct stand in opposition to the Know-Nothings.[19] There was no serious doubt at any time as to the outcome of the election in 1856. Some of the old Whigs did not favor the new Republican party, and the German press remained faithful to the Democrats; but the Know-Nothing party practically collapsed, its followers joining the ranks of the Republicans.[20] The Democrats were not able to survive the controversies within their own ranks, which had remained since 1854; the Pierce administration was not popular in Iowa, and, as in other states, Buchanan was held up as a servant of the "slave power." The Kansas issue and the personal popularity of Frémont were also decidedly influencial factors in the campaign in that state.[21]

---

[15] They were the *California Demokrat* and the *San Francisco Journal*. See *Detroit Free Press*, August 20, 1856.

[16] This was the fact that the free-soil element had been thrust in the background.

[17] Pelzer, "The Origin and Organization of the Republican Party in Iowa," *Iowa Journal of History and Politics*, IV, 490.

[18] Christoferson, Life of Grimes, p. 120, MS, University of Iowa.

[19] Pelzer, *op. cit.*, p. 494.

[20] *Ibid.*, p. 495.

[21] *Iowa City Republican*, June 26, 1856. See also issue of June 9, 1856.

In Iowa a Republican victory was fairly certain from the outset; but in the neighboring state, Illinois, the situation presented a fairly even opportunity for the success of either major party. The Republicans held their first meeting at Decatur on February 22, but the attendance was small and the conservative temper of the leaders of the party was shown by the resolutions on the slavery question.[22] The state convention met at Bloomington May 29; but, even then, thirty of the southern counties of the state were not represented, and the resolutions which were adopted were no more radical than those of the former meeting.[23]

The Know-Nothing party was of importance in Illinois, for many of the old-time Whigs supported Fillmore because they did not like Frémont.[24] Lincoln had urged the selection of McLean in place of Frémont because he believed that in case of the selection of the latter the Whigs would vote for Buchanan.[25] Herndon, however, believed that although the Whigs disliked Frémont enough to vote for Buchanan they would not do so since they had Fillmore to vote for.[26] Thus the Whig support of Fillmore encouraged the Know-Nothings, and if the Republicans should make a direct bid for the support of that group by giving its followers places on the state party ticket[27] or by some other means, there was danger of losing whatever chance the party had of getting the German vote, which was thought to be absolutely essential for success in the election, and which, of course, was anti-Know-Nothing.[28]

Lincoln undoubtedly found it difficult to support Frémont. "The great difficulty," he said, "with all antislavery extension Fillmore men, is that they suppose Fillmore as good as Frémont on that question; and it is a delicate point

[22] Cole, *Era of the Civil War* (Centennial History of Illinois, III), p. 143.

[23] *Ibid.*, p. 144.

[24] Rankin, *Reminiscences*, p. 205.

[25] Lincoln to Trumbull, June 7, 1856; quoted in Tracy, *Uncollected Letters of Abraham Lincoln*, p. 67.

[26] Herndon to Trumbull, July 12, 1856. Trumbull MSS.

[27] C. H. Ray to Trumbull, March 21, 1856. Trumbull MSS. Ray estimated that there were 20,000 German voters in Illinois who must be induced to vote for Frémont.

[28] *Ibid.*

to argue them out of it; they are so ready to think you are abusing Mr. Fillmore."[29]   Other leaders besides Lincoln found it difficult to unite the anti-Nebraska men behind the Frémont movement. It was said that many such men thought that Frémont possessed neither the character nor the talents to command the respect of the people.[30]

There were other views, however, concerning Frémont. According to Rankin, the law office of Herndon and Lincoln at Springfield was substantially the Republican headquarters during the campaign.[31]   In that case Herndon should have been able to observe the situation correctly, and he believed that the selection of Frémont was the "wisest choice that could have been made under all circumstances," although he had not thought so at first.[32]   In the northern part of the state where the keynote of the party was conservatism and a middle-of-the-way attitude, Frémont found favor because he was an available man.[33]   At any rate, if the Frémont candidacy alienated from the party no other group but the old Whigs, such an alienation was comparatively unimportant, for it was an even chance at least that they would support Fillmore instead of Buchanan.

The German voters of the state were ardently sought by both major parties, German speakers being employed to defend each side. Francis J. Grund, defending the Democrats, declared that they favored the foreign-born, they defended the Catholics, and they openly denounced the Know-Nothings.   The Republicans, he said, were Yankees who cheated honest farmers by selling them worthless lightning rods, and who, being temperance advocates, would prevent the Germans from drinking beer on Sunday.[34]   Gustave Koerner replied to Grund, but the oratorical contest developed into personalities.   Many of the prominent Germans remained aloof from the campaign,[35] and at the end the

---

[29] Lincoln to Trumbull, August 11, 1856; quoted in Tracy, *op. cit.*, p. 70.

[30] B. S. Edwards to Trumbull, July 24, 1856. Trumbull MSS.

[31] Rankin, *Recollections*, p. 27.

[32] Herndon to Trumbull, July 12, 1856. Trumbull MSS.

[33] Koerner, *Recollections*, II, 26.

[34] *Ibid.*   [35] Cole, *Era of the Civil War*, p. 149.

Republicans did not claim that they had been able to secure the support of very many of the Catholic Germans.[36]

Notwithstanding the various difficulties, the campaign for Frémont was carried on with vigor; although a few Republicans thought that it was wanting in force.[37] The lack of money and printed matter was deplored on all sides.[38] Long afterward an observer declared that it was the most bitterly contested campaign that he remembered in fifty years.[39] The most prominent men who spoke for Frémont were John P. Hale, Nathaniel P. Banks, Anson Burlingame, Owen Lovejoy, and John M. Palmer.[40]

The main issue was the Kansas question. The report of the Kansas investigating committee was distributed throughout the state, and emigrants who had returned from Kansas were used to keep the story of "bleeding Kansas" before the people. A favorite method of obtaining an audience was to hold a barbecue, after which followed the speeches.[41] Logan, in his *Recollections*, declared that practically every man in southern Illinois thought that he knew all about the questions involved in the contest; and therefore at all public gatherings and meetings "multitudes assembled, men and women flocked to political demonstrations as they would to a camp meeting or to a circus."[42] Processions, pageants, and bands enlivened the occasions.

There were many people in Illinois, however, whose heads were not turned by the Kansas reports. They recognized that the conduct of the proslavery party in Kansas was indefensible, but that at the same time the acts of the antislavery party were likewise indefensible. "I fear for my country," declared one writer, "because I see nobody in it with the necessary character and influence who is willing

---

[36] Koerner, *Recollections*, II, 21.
[37] F. S. Rutherford to Trumbull, July 21, 1856. Trumbull MSS.
[38] Koerner to Trumbull, July 29, 1856; Brown to Trumbull, July 28, 1856. Trumbull MSS.
[39] Rankin, *Recollections*, p. 206.
[40] Cole, *Era of the Civil War*, p. 147.
[41] Logan, *Recollections*, pp. 50 ff., contains a good description of one of these gatherings.
[42] *Ibid.*, p. 55.

to save it.   Here is a festering sore which requires mild treatment to heal it, yet no one stands ready with a cruit of oil to dress the wound, but all are pouring on vitteral and emulous only to see who can aggravate it the most."[43]   This writer believed that Fillmore was probably best fitted to heal the nation's wounds, but since he could not be elected, and since Frémont did not have the force of character or positive influence to accomplish any good result, it remained for patriots to vote for Buchanan.   Many of the old Clay Whigs began to sense the essential nationalistic position of the Democratic party,[44] and it was believed that Lincoln and Judge Davis were the only prominent Whigs in the central part of the state who remained faithful to Frémont.[45]

Herndon declared that it was extremely difficult to get together the fragments of factions and odds and ends of parties in a concerted movement for Frémont.[46]   It was almost impossible to get the Know-Nothing support, partly because it was believed by many people that Frémont was a Catholic.[47]   In the northern part of the state Frémont proved to be a good candidate, but he was not particularly popular elsewhere, and the clear-sighted observers realized that the anti-Nebraska forces were disorganized, and that defeat for the Republicans was inevitable.[48]

The campaign in Indiana began with the meeting of the Democratic state convention at Indianapolis in January. The party resolutions adopted there declared approval of the Kansas-Nebraska Act, and opposed Know-Nothingism and prohibition laws, as well as further restriction on the naturalization of foreigners.[49] The Democrats of Indiana had opposed the Know-Nothing organization from the beginning, and as a consequence many Whigs had drifted into the

---

[43] J. D. Caton to Trumbull, July 3, 1856. Trumbull MSS.
[44] Cole, *Era of the Civil War*, p. 149.
[45] Koerner, *Recollections*, II, 22.
[46] Herndon to Trumbull, July 29, 1856. Trumbull MSS.
[47] George Allen to Trumbull, July, 1856. Trumbull MSS.
[48] Richard Gates to Trumbull, August 3, 1856. Trumbull MSS.
[49] Zimmerman, "Origin and Rise of Republican Party in Indiana," *Indiana Magazine of History*, XIII, 249.

Know-Nothing party.[50] That party, therefore, was of great importance in the Indiana situation, its leaders believing that it could muster fifty thousand votes.[51]

The Indiana Know-Nothings, however, were inclined toward fusion with the Republicans, and their state committee sent out a call to all members of the party to send delegates to the "People's Convention" which was to be held in May.[52] The first duty of the Republicans, therefore, was to conduct the convention in such a manner as to secure the good will of the Know-Nothings. This was attempted by the adoption of a formal resolution favoring the prohibition of suffrage to unnaturalized foreigners.[53]

Wherever it was attempted, the fusion of the Know-Nothings and Republicans was a difficult task. Indiana was no exception. The Republicans had no thought of letting the Frémont movement appear as Know-Nothingism under a different name, and consequently only one Know-Nothing was placed on the fusion state ticket.[54] As a result, many of the Know-Nothings, being dissatisfied, decided to hold a state convention of their own.[55] This convention, although it did not put a state ticket in the field, declared support of Fillmore and was clearly of the opinion that the fusionists were Republicans in disguise.[56]

It seems clear that the Republicans of Indiana were timid. They were afraid on the one hand of losing the Know-Nothing support and on the other of losing that of the Germans; and they desired to be anti-Nebraska in character and yet to avoid the appearance of abolitionism. The fusion leaders hesitated to send antislavery speakers into the southern districts of the state for fear of doing more damage than

---

[50] Brand, "The Know-Nothing Party in Indiana," *Indiana Magazine of History*, XVIII, 69.
[51] *Indianapolis Journal*, March 7, 1856.
[52] *Ibid.*, April 11, 1856.
[53] *Ibid.*, May 8, 1856.   [54] *Ibid.*, May 8, 1856.
[55] The convention met at Indianapolis, July 16, 1856.
[56] *Weekly State Journal*, July 24, 1856.
[57] H. S. Lane, the President of the Republican state convention, made it clear that there was no taint of abolitionism about the new party. *Weekly State Journal*, May 8, 1856.

good.[58] "Our State," wrote Julian to Chase, "is not at all like Ohio, and I am sorry I could not convince you of this when I last saw you. We have a very mean scurvy pack of politicians in our so-called Republican party—doughfaces at heart— whose knavery for the past two years has been greatly facilitated by Know-Nothingism."[59]

Since the Know-Nothings did not have a state ticket it was evident that the election of state officers which was held in October would be a test of strength. Although the contest was close, the Democratic candidate for governor won the election by over five thousand votes.[60] This result practically ended all hope of Frémont's election; his most ardent advocates practically gave up the contest.[61]

A few of the die-hard Frémonters thought that the Know-Nothings had double-crossed the fusion candidates in the state election by voting for the Democrats, and that in the national elections they would vote for Fillmore, and therefore Frémont might profit by that change.[62] This, however, was not the case. The majority of the Fillmore journals had already deserted to the Frémont camp,[63] and in the presidential election Frémont received over seventeen thousand votes less than the fusion candidate for governor, while the Democratic vote remained practically the same in each election.[64] At any rate, whatever shifting may have taken place, Frémont derived no benefit from it.

In Ohio the outcome of the election depended largely on the ability of the Frémont leaders to hold together the political factions that had united in the election of Chase to the governorship in 1855. In the fall of that year Chase believed that the aid of the liberal Know-Nothings and the antislavery "adopted citizens" would be necessary for Republican success in the presidential election. "The problem,"

---

[58] *Ibid.*

[59] George W. Julian to Chase, July 22, 1856. Chase MSS (Pa. Hist. Soc.).

[60] Brand, *op. cit.*, p. 284.

[61] *Ibid.*, p. 281. Hollister, *Colfax*, p. 104.

[62] Zimmerman, *op. cit.*, p. 265.   [63] *Ibid.*

[64] The complete election returns and comparison of votes are given in Brand, *op. cit.*, pp. 291 ff.

he declared, "is to reconcile the two, and I see no way in which it can be done except by liberalizing the creed and declaration of the former, or by a nomination acceptable enough on each side to secure general acquiescence. Besides these classes we needs must have a large acceptance from the Democratic element."[65]

Chase thought that since he had harmonized those elements in Ohio in 1855 he was the logical candidate for the presidency,[66] but he supported Frémont and spoke on occasion throughout Ohio.[67] On the other hand, McLean took no part in the campaign. He had no confidence in Frémont and believed that both he and his friends were dishonest politicians.[68] The *Cincinnati Gazette* declared very frankly that the great aim of the Republicans was to defeat the Democratic party; and, second to that, it was desirable to elect a president who opposed the spread of slavery into new areas.[69] The Ohio Republicans, of course, had not been ardent advocates of Frémont's nomination.

The Know-Nothings held their state convention at Columbus, March 20, but party harmony was lacking. The majority of the convention was in sympathy with the action of the Ohio delegates in seceding from the national convention, while the minority, about thirty-six out of one hundred and eighty delegates, was inclined to support Fillmore.[70] The convention passed resolutions which clearly indicated that fusion with the Republicans was intended; the declaration on the American question simply demanded freedom of religion and equality of rights for naturalized citizens. Although the president of the Know-Nothing Order denounced the convention, he created a new council for Ohio and called a convention to meet at Columbus on May 27;[71] but only a few people attended, and the *Cleveland Herald* spoke of

---

[65] Chase to K. S. Bingham, October 19, 1865. Chase MSS (Pa. Hist. Soc.).
[66] *Ibid.*   [67] *New York Tribune,* July 4, 1856.
[68] John McLean to Teesdale, September 3, 1859. Teesdale, *McLean Letters,* p. 240.
[69] February 27, 1856.
[70] *Cleveland Herald,* March 21, 1856; *Ohio State Journal,* March 21, 1856.
[71] *Ohio State Journal,* March 23, 1856.

the Fillmore movement in Ohio as not in reality a "movement but a squirming."[72]

The campaign in Ohio possessed few if any unique features. Anson Burlingame, C. M. Clay, Chase, and R. P. Spaulding were among the most prominent Frémont speakers. James A. Garfield, then a teacher at Hiram College, entered the campaign and spoke forty times.[73] Mass meetings were held *ad infinitum;* it was said that sixty-one county mass meetings were held.[74] At a great meeting in Sandusky, held on the anniversary of Perry's victory, an estimated throng of twenty-five thousand people witnessed a performance arranged to depict the action of Missouri "border ruffians." Three hundred men rode in a body from Tiffin to Frémont, Ohio, to attend a similar meeting at which a wagon filled with girls and drawn by eighteen pairs of white horses was the feature of the day.

The appeal for Frémont votes was much the same as elsewhere; the denunciation of the South, the Kansas outrages, and the Brooks-Sumner affair made up the raw material for campaign orators.[75] The press of the state was predominatingly Republican and the prospects for Frémont's success there were bright indeed.

The campaign for Frémont in Michigan was waged with no less vigor or success than in Ohio. The Democrats sent Lewis Cass and John Van Buren into the southern part of the state, Stephen A. Douglas and Daniel Dickinson of New York into the central areas, and John C. Breckinridge, Colonel Preston of Kentucky, and Jesse D. Bright of Indiana into various places.[76] The most important Republican speakers were J. M. and W. A. Howard, Zachariah Chandler, and Austin Blair.

The Republicans took high ground on the Kansas question, even to the extent of justifying civil war against the

[72] July 30, 1856.

[73] Smith, *Life of Garfield*, I, 122.

[74] *Cleveland Herald*, September 11, 1856.

[75] See Chase's speech at Cincinnati, quoted in *Ohio State Journal*, July 8, or in *Cincinnati Gazette*, August 3, 1856; also *New York Tribune*, July 4, 1856.

[76] Stocking, *Under the Oakes, passim,* contains a summary of the campaign.

proslavery settlers of Kansas.[77] On the other hand, the Democrats presented an example of that party in its most conservative mood.[78] The state convention adopted resolutions which deprecated the idea of secession in case of a Republican victory and pledged fidelity to the Union,[79] while the only stand on the Kansas issue was to declare support for the Toombs Bill.[80]

The most widely heralded speech of the Frémont party during the campaign was made by Seward at Detroit, October 2, one of the few speeches made by him during the campaign.[81] The import of the address was to show that a comparatively small number of Southern slave owners controlled Congress, its committees and legislation, the Cabinet, and, in short, the whole government. This control was exercised mainly for one purpose, slavery extension. The Democratic press noted that the address was a denunciation of a section rather than a defense of a party,[82] and even some Republican journals were inclined to find fault with the tone of the speech.[83]

The Democrats made an attempt to secure Whig support by the conservative attitude on the sectional question,[84] and by emphasizing the sectional character of the Republicans.[85] The Know-Nothing movement was of no serious concern to either party.[86] Local issues were of some importance, the most prominent being the temperance law which the Demo-

---

[77] *Detroit Free Press*, March 28, 1856.
[78] As shown by the resolutions of the party convention. *Detroit Free Press*, March 22, 1856.
[79] This was done both at the convention to select national convention delegates, and at the state nominating convention. See *Detroit Free Press*, March 22 and August 8, 1856, for the latter meeting.
[80] *Detroit Free Press*, October 7, 1856.
[81] It was printed by many journals, among them the *Detroit Free Press*, October 7, and the *New York Tribune*, October 3.
[82] *Detroit Free Press*, October 30, 1856; *Daily News*, October 8, 1856.
[83] *New York Herald*; quoted in *Daily News, loc. cit.*
[84] *Detroit Free Press*, August 23, 1856. See also Streeter, *Political Parties in Michigan*, p. 203.
[85] *Detroit Free Press*, August 9, 1856.
[86] The *Ann Arbor Register* supported Fillmore, but a meeting held in Detroit, October 2, to consider putting a ticket into the field was a complete failure. *Ibid.*, September 4 and October 3, 1856.

crats desired to replace with a license system.[87] The latter made a final effort to rally their forces after the October elections in Pennsylvania,[88] but the success of Frémont in Michigan was a foregone conclusion.

The movement for Frémont did not take root in the South. In August an attempt was made to hold a Frémont meeting at Wheeling, Virginia, but a mob was formed and the meeting broken up. The *Wheeling Daily News* declared that while there were a good many people in that area who looked upon slavery as an evil and favored peaceful and gradual emancipation, the leaders of the attempted Frémont meeting were abolitionists who would do more harm than good.[89] About a month later another Frémont meeting was held at Wheeling, calling itself the "Republican State Convention of Virginia."[90] No disturbance of any kind attended this gathering, and it proceeded to pass resolutions in opposition to the extension of slavery.[91] This meeting received some comment from the Northern press, which talked of a Frémont party in Virginia, but the *Richmond Enquirer* asserted that this affair had been sponsored by the Fillmore party and that to all intents and purposes there was no Frémont ticket in Virginia.[92] Aside from this insignificant movement, the contest in the South was between Fillmore and Buchanan.

James Buchanan was not the first choice of the Southern delegates at the Cincinnati convention, but he had the ardent support of a few of them and was not particularly objectionable to the rest.[93] His nomination found considerable favor with the Whigs of the South. "If we are destined to have another Democratic President," declared the Whig *Baltimore Patriot*, "it will be some satisfaction to feel that, of all the candidates put in nomination for that exalted office, Mr.

---

[87] *Detroit Free Press*, March 30, April 19, October 28, 1856.
[88] *Ibid.*, October 28, 1856.
[89] *Wheeling Daily News*, August 18, 1856.
[90] *New York Tribune*, October 1, 1856.
[91] *New York Herald*, September 19, 1856.
[92] Quoted in *Charleston* (S. C.) *Courier*, September 16, 1856.
[93] See *Richmond Enquirer*, June 9, 1856, for Southern opinion of his nomination.

Buchanan is more likely to prove the least objectionable."[94]
The *Richmond Whig* declared that for the first time the
Democrats had approached the Whigs in the character of
their candidate.[95]

At the same time Fillmore was essentially a Southern
candidate, since it was the Northern wing of the Know-
Nothing party that had seceded from the national convention.
In an address at Albany, at the outset of the campaign, Fillmore sharply denounced the Republican party for its sec-
tionalism and intimated that in case of a Republican victory
the South would be justified in secession.[96] As a consequence,
it was pointed out in the North that only those who had
proslavery tendencies could support Fillmore,[97] while in the
South the address was well received.[98] On the Kansas-
Nebraska question, however, Fillmore did not quite measure
up to Southern expectations. Speaking at Rochester he declared that the Kansas-Nebraska Act did not arise in the
South and that, however much its passage might be deplored,
it afforded no just reason for Northern hostility toward the
South.[99] This was a middle-of-the-road position and was
widely used against him with more or less effect by the
Buchanan journals.

The whole crux of the Fillmore candidacy was well
stated by Thurlow Weed: "Fillmore's nomination will im-
pose upon the Democratic party the necessity of contesting
every Southern state."[100] It was patent that, in case of a close
contest in the North, the result of the campaign might depend on a comparatively few Southern electoral votes. Thus,
a Fillmore victory in a few states might turn the balance for
Frémont or throw the election into the House.

The Fillmore following was composed of Whigs, Know-
Nothings, and various other men who for one reason or

---

[94] Quoted in *Richmond Enquirer*, June 9, 1856.   [95] *Ibid.*
[96] *Ohio State Journal*, July 3, 1856; *Baltimore American*, June 30, 1856.
[97] *Ohio State Journal*, July 1, 1856.
[98] John Tyler to J. S. Cunningham, July 14, 1856; quoted in Tyler, *Letters and Times of the Tylers*, II, 530. See also *Ohio State Journal*, July 5, 1856.
[99] *Baltimore American*, July 2, 1856.
[100] Weed to W. M. Marcey, Mar. 7, 1856. William S. Marcey MSS.

another were dissatisfied with the Democrats.[101] The appeal for him was made mostly on the basis of the moderate and conservative character of his position. The *Baltimore American* put his case very clearly: "He is, in the most elevated sense of the word, the compromise candidate for the presidency—a candidate not committed by affiliation with the extremes of either section, but standing upon national ground for national purposes, is equally acceptable to both, and in the best position to bring about that accord which may rob the quarrel of its irritable causes and pave the way to settlement and peace."[102] Patriots who would preserve the Union from wreck and dissolution were urged to follow Fillmore.[103]

The Democrats could make the same kind of appeal for Buchanan, for he too was a conservative candidate. This fact, however, while a source of party strength in the North, caused some embarrassment in the South. Fillmore journals found statements made by Buchanan which indicated that he was not a friend of the institution of slavery,[104] and the best answer that the *Richmond Enquirer* could make was that he had never opposed the constitutional guaranties of that institution.[105] A presidential candidate whose personal opinions might be hostile to slavery could not expect great popularity in the Southern states. Andrew Johnson of Tennessee declared that Buchanan was less easy to defend than any other prominent Democrat who had been considered as a possible candidate.[106]

The success of Fillmore in the South depended on his ability to gain the support of all the old Whigs and at the same time retain his nominal Know-Nothing following. This did not seem to be an impossible task; the Southern state

---

[101] Stirling, *Letters from the Slave States*, p. 88; *Savannah Republican*, July 26, 1856, gives an analysis of the situation. See also Cole, *The Whig Party in the South*, *passim*.

[102] *Baltimore American*, June 26, 1856.

[103] *Ibid.*, August 26, 1856.

[104] *Daily Constitutionalist* (Augusta), June 2, 1856.

[105] *Richmond Enquirer*, June 20, 1856.

[106] Johnson to W. M. Lowery, June 26, 1856; also Johnson to R. C. Johnson, June 28, 1856. Andrew Johnson MSS.

elections had been very closely contested by the Know-Nothings, and in two states Know-Nothing governors were elected.[107] Moreover, the Albany speech had been well received by Southern Whigs,[108] and it was stated that seven-eighths of the Whigs were willing to support Fillmore.[109] Nevertheless, since he was nominally a Know-Nothing candidate, his friends planned to have the Whigs formally accept him as their candidate. In consequence, a Whig state convention was held at Richmond, Virginia, July 16,[110] and other state Whig conventions were held throughout the South.[111] Eventually a Whig national convention was organized at Baltimore.[112] It was generally understood that the purpose of the convention was to nominate Fillmore.

The test of the Fillmore strength in the South came in Kentucky. That state had been carried by the Whigs in 1852, and by the Know-Nothings in 1855.[113] The Democrats appealed to the voters to support Buchanan on the grounds that Southern solidity was necessary to insure the defeat of the Republicans.[114] Of course, the Know-Nothings countered with the assertion that the election of Frémont could be prevented only by a Fillmore victory,[115] but the Democratic appeal had considerable force, and, with a few notable exceptions, the most important Fillmore leaders joined the Buchanan forces.[116] As a result the state election in August was a Democratic triumph.

[107] See *Tribune Almanac*, 1856. The two states were Texas and Kentucky.

[108] John Tyler to Cunningham; quoted in Tyler, *Times of the Tylers*, II, 530.

[109] *Louisiana Courier*, August 3, 1856.

[110] *Richmond Enquirer*, July 18, 1856; *New York Tribune*, July 18, 1856; *Republican Banner* (Nashville), July 25, 1856. The convention denounced both the Republicans and the Democrats, but the character of the meeting was seen when it failed to pass a resolution declaring itself exclusively Whig.

[111] At the Kentucky meeting only a few Whigs were present. See *Louisville Times*, September 9, 1856; The *Louisiana Courier*, August 3, 1856, reported a Whig meeting at New Orleans. See also *Florida News*, May 19, 1856.

[112] See below, p. 59.

[113] *Tribune Almanac*, 1856.

[114] P. L. Letcher to Crittenden, July 30, 1856, Crittenden MSS; *Louisville Times*, June 25, 26, July 2, 16, 1856.

[115] P. L. Letcher to Crittenden, July 1 and also July 30, 1856, Crittenden MSS; *Baltimore American*, July 26, 1856.

[116] Barton M. Clay and Colonel Preston were among those who deserted Fillmore. See *New York Tribune*, August 7, 1856; also Cole, *Whig Party in the South*, p. 325.

Next to Kentucky, Tennessee probably presented the most favorable situation for a Fillmore victory. Early in the year, W. G. Brownlow declared that the state could be carried for anyone who opposed the Democrats;[117] and Andrew Johnson, complaining that there was little enthusiasm for Buchanan,[118] believed that if the Know-Nothings were well organized they would be successful. The *Republican Banner* of Nashville, one of the most ardent Fillmore journals of the South, searched the public record of Buchanan and published an account of every act which might give color to the charge that he favored high tariffs or popular sovereignty, or opposed slavery.[119] But the failure of Fillmore in Kentucky, the fear of a Frémont victory, and the lack of unity in the Fillmore ranks made the election a Democratic triumph.

In other Southern states there was less chance of a Fillmore victory than there was in Kentucky and Tennessee. In Louisiana the Democrats sought to smooth out the factional difficulties, to conciliate the discordant elements of the state, and to appeal to the necessity of maintaining a solid front against a Northern sectional party.[120] In Georgia the candidacy of Fillmore was not popular. To be sure, some Fillmore meetings were held,[121] but many of the old Whigs came to the support of Buchanan,[122] and the ardent support given to the latter by Toombs, Stephens, Cobb, and Troup was an important factor.[123] The fear of disunion was especially prominent in Georgia, the Fillmore journals admitting that disunion would follow the success of Frémont.[124]

By the end of September, Fillmore realized that his chance of success in the South was very small. "After all I have done," he said, "and all the sacrifice I have made to

---

[117] W. G. Brownlow to Bell, January 15, 1856. John Bell MSS.

[118] Johnson to W. M. Lowery, June 26, 1856. Andrew Johnson MSS.

[119] See June 19, 20, July 26, August 8, 1856.

[120] See Speech of W. S. Parkham at Baton Rouge, *Louisiana Courier,* September 9, 21, 24, October 31, 1856.

[121] *Savannah Republican,* July 7, 1856.

[122] See Fielden, *Sketch of Life of Brown,* p. 81.

[123] Phillips, *Georgia and State Rights,* p. 179; also Fielden, *op. cit.,* p. 80.

[124] *Savannah Republican,* August 26, 1856.

maintain the constitutional rights of the South, she still dis-
trusts me."[125] It is at least doubtful that the South distrusted
Fillmore personally, but it did fear a Frémont victory. The
Richmond Enquirer may have voiced the sentiment of most
Southerners when it said that even if Fillmore was as capable
as Buchanan, and even if Whigs disliked to support a Democrat, still, when independence and liberty were the issues,
patriotic Southern men could not neglect their duty.[126]

---

[125] Quoted in *New York Tribune*, October 13, 1856.

[126] *Richmond Enquirer*, August 13, 1856; this sentiment was stated in various
ways all over the South. See *Nashville Times*, October 26; *Charleston Courier*, September 24; *St. Louis Pilot*, September 16; *National Era*, August 23; *Daily Globe*,
August 15; *New York Tribune*, August 7; *New York Times*, August 26; also Cole,
Whig Party in the South, p. 325.

CHAPTER V

THE CAMPAIGN IN THE NORTH

While the campaign was being waged in the South and West, it was being conducted in the North with no less enthusiasm and earnestness. McClure of Pennsylvania spoke of it as a "tidal wave of impulsive politics."[1] James Walker declared that one could "scarcely conceive the intense bitterness" which it engendered in Rhode Island,[2] and a man of such political experience as Martin Van Buren believed that the crisis was "the most imminent and critical" that the country had experienced.[3] Buchanan believed that the "preachers and fanatics" of New England had so excited the people on the question of slavery that they prayed and preached for Frémont's election.[4] On this election, declared Thomas Ruffin, the "salvation of the country depends,"[5] and Samuel Bowles thought that he had never lived in "times like these before."[6] These expressions, be it noted, come from private correspondence and not from public declamation and therefore probably express the real conviction of the writers.

The sharp divergence of opinion as set down by two foreigners in the United States shows, as well as anything could, the marked and almost illimitable diversion of view that existed. "It may, indeed, be said of the Republican Party," one visitor wrote, "that it consisted of all that was best in all other parties. It contained the most liberal Whigs and the most conservative Democrats. It was a party, in

---

[1] McClure, *Pennsylvania*, I, 264.
[2] James Walker to Chase, September 22, 1856. Chase MSS.
[3] Van Buren to Moses Tilden, September 1, 1856; quoted in Bigelow, *Tilden*, I, 119.
[4] Buchanan to Bates, November 6, 1856 (Copy). Buchanan MSS.
[5] Thomas Ruffin to Ruffin, August 28, 1856; quoted in Hamilton, *Ruffin Papers*, II, 518.
[6] Bowles to Charles Allen, August 22, 1856; quoted in Merriman, *Bowles*, I, 157 ff.

short, of all those party men who were above mere party.
. . . Those noble sons of noble sires are the true Democracy
of the Western world, and will rescue popular government
from the contempt and derision which the spurious, self-
styled Democrats of the South would put upon it."[7] The
other foreigner, after visiting the House of Representatives
and listening to the speeches of Republican members, wrote:
"They seemed to be either grim and ghastly fanatics, fellows
raving about slavery, or mere corrupt and mercenary politicians, ready to run the ship of state upon the breakers, and
then plunder the wreck; to set the house on fire and run away
with the spoons."[8]

The outcome of the campaign in the East and North
depended, as it did elsewhere, on the degree of organization
that could be infused into the Republican party and on the
action of the Whigs and Know-Nothings. The issues in the
campaign were the same there as elsewhere, but the Whig-
Fillmore movement and the details of the campaign deserve
separate treatment.

There were several organizations of Whigs in 1856 calling themselves "Pure Whigs," "Unchanged Whigs,"
"Straight Whigs," or "Unfused Whigs."[9] If these Whigs
and Know-Nothings could be added to the regular Republican fold, their success would seem certain.[10] Many of the
Whigs were undecided, and at best there was a lack of unity
among them. For example, James A. Hamilton was disposed to overlook the fact that Fillmore was running on a
Know-Nothing platform and to consider him essentially as
a Whig candidate whom the Whigs, by the action of a
national convention, should nominate, and who, once nominated in such a manner, would draw away from the Republicans their Whig adherents. "As a National Whig," he said,
"and a citizen feeling a lively interest in the welfare of the
country, I am disposed to support the nomination [Fillmore]

[7] Stirling, *Slave States*, p. 82.
[8] Nicholas, *Forty Years in the United States*, I, 259.
[9] *New York Tribune*, March 24, 1856.
[10] *New York Herald*, February 27, 1856; *New York Tribune*, February 27, 1856.

because I believe it the safest and best that will be presented to our choice."[11]   On the other hand, Hamilton Fish looked upon Fillmore as essentially a Know-Nothing.   He declared that he did not see his way clear to support the Know-Nothing candidates in consideration of the platform upon which they were presented.   He did not like Donelson, who had opposed the Whigs, and so he thought a Whig convention impracticable.[12]

Edward Everett, another old Whig, believed that the majority of the Whigs of Massachusetts would vote for Fillmore, and declared that he would do so himself.   He doubted that Fillmore could carry the state because the majority of the Know-Nothing party, originally Free-Soilers, had united with the Republicans.[13]   The case of John Winthrop is a good illustration of the dilemma in which many Whigs found themselves.   He said that at times he thought he would support Frémont, and at other times Buchanan.   Yet he could not bring himself to the point of giving aid to a sectional party or support to the Democrats, whom he had opposed so long, and so he concluded that, as far as he was concerned personally, it was best to support Fillmore.[14]

On the other hand, some of the old Whigs decided to support Buchanan.   Although this was especially the case in Pennsylvania,[15] it prevailed elsewhere; Rufus Choate may be taken as an outstanding example.   In an address at Lowell, Massachusetts, he deplored the sectional strife, which, he said, had been engendered by a party that talked of peace and order while it refused to permit such a condition to come about save at its own instance and under its control.   He believed, therefore, that if the Republicans really desired peace and freedom in Kansas they could have it by support-

---

[11] Hamilton to Hamilton Fish, March 7, 1856; quoted in James A. Hamilton, *Reminiscences*, p. 410.

[12] Fish to J. A. Hamilton, March 4, 1856.   Hamilton, *Reminiscences*, pp. 408-10.

[13] Edward Everett to J. A. Hamilton, June 30, 1856.   Hamilton, *Reminiscences*, p. 412.

[14] Winthrop, *Memoirs of Winthrop*, pp. 186-87.

[15] McClure: *Recollections*, p. 441; and *Notes on Pennsylvania*, pp. 248-51.

ing the Toombs Bill; at any rate, since a sectional party contemplated an injustice to the section which it excluded, he would support the national party and Buchanan.[16] There were a good many business men among the Whigs, who, like Choate, opposed a sectional party or feared secession and therefore supported Buchanan.[17] "The first duty, then, of Whigs," declared a Boston Whig, "not merely as patriots and citizens—loving with a large and equal love our whole native land—but as Whigs, and because we are Whigs, is to unite with some organization of our countrymen to defeat and dissolve the new geographical party, calling itself Republican."[18]

After all is said, however, it is probable that the majority of the Whigs in the North joined the Frémont movement. On the whole it was easier for a Whig to join a new movement than an old one which had been opposed to Whiggery for many years. A Connecticut Whig declared that Fillmore's speech at Albany made him an impossible candidate; and since Buchanan, a Democrat, could not be supported, the only course open for the Whigs was to vote for Frémont.[19] When the campaign was over, a New York observer believed that at least a hundred thousand Whigs of that state had voted for Frémont.[20]

The Fillmore leaders were aware that there were some Whigs in the North who did not wish to support either Frémont or Buchanan and yet were undecided as to whether it would be worth while to support Fillmore.[21] They decided, therefore, to sponsor a Whig national convention which would nominate Fillmore as a Whig candidate. This movement was organized and the convention met at Baltimore,

---

[16] Of course this is a paraphrase of a long speech. It is printed in full in *Daily Union*, November 1, 1856.

[17] See Smith, *Political History of Slavery*, I, 338.

[18] This was E. W. Farley, writing to the Whig State Committee of Maine, August 9, 1856; quoted in Brown, *Works of Choate*, I, 212. Thomas G. Pratt of Maryland assumed a similar position and others did likewise. See *Democratic Campaign Documents* for further examples.

[19] G. P. Marsh to C. D. Drake (1856); quoted in Marsh, *Life of Marsh*, p. 379.

[20] C. D. Davis to Marcey, November 13, 1856. Marcey MSS.

[21] See for example, G. T. Curtis to Crittenden, July 3, 1856. Crittenden MSS.

September 17, 1856.[22] Washington Hunt, of Kentucky, in the opening speech, deplored sectional parties; he asserted that the Whig party still existed, and took high ground against the Republicans.[23] There does not seem to be any evidence, however, that this convention stimulated any Fillmore support that he did not have already.[24]

Among the Eastern states the earliest state election was held in Maine. A great amount of interest centered in that election because Maine was one state where the Whigs still maintained a certain solidarity.[25] Although the Republicans, with the aid, it was thought, of sixteen thousand Whigs, had carried the state in 1855,[26] it was known that many of the latter did not like Frémont,[27] and the Democrats had been very careful not to take a radical stand on the slavery issue, confining themselves simply to supporting the idea of popular sovereignty.[28] The Republicans, on the other hand, were particularly fortunate in having an exceptionally popular candidate for the governorship in the person of Hannibal Hamlin. That fact, together with the ardent efforts of Israel Washburn and Pike, and the financial support which was secured through Thurlow Weed, carried the state for Frémont.[29]

The political situation in Connecticut was not particularly complicated. The Know-Nothing convention which met at Hartford July 9, decided to support Frémont,[30] and the

---

[22] *Baltimore American,* September 18, 1856.

[23] *New York Herald,* September 18, 1856. For the resolutions which asserted about what Hunt had declared in his speech see *New York Herald,* September 19.

[24] McClure, *Notes on Pennsylvania,* I, 244; Cole, *Whig Party in the South,* p. 326; Smith, *Political History of Slavery,* I, 230; McMaster, *History of United States,* VIII, 265.

[25] At a Whig state convention held at Bangor early in July there were three or four hundred delegates. See the *Age* (Augusta), July 10, 1856.

[26] *New York Tribune,* September 9, 1856.

[27] See letters to Pike from Dana and Greeley; quoted in Pike, *First Blows of the Civil War,* pp. 337 ff.

[28] The *Age* (Augusta), July 10, 1856.

[29] Israel Washburn to John Stevens, July 5, August 16, 1856. Israel Washburn MSS. See letter quoted in Pike, *First Blows of the Civil War,* pp. 337 ff; the *Age,* July 12, August 10, 1856.

[30] *New York Times,* July 11, 1856. There were a few Know-Nothings who did not like this action, who met in a separate convention at Hartford, and nominated Fillmore. See *New York Tribune,* July 11, 1856.

Republicans who had selected a former Democrat, Gideon Welles, as their candidate for the governorship, were enabled to present a united opposition to Buchanan, and to carry the state for Frémont.[31]

The political situation in Massachusetts was likewise devoid of special features. The situation there was succinctly stated by John Winthrop. "Between ourselves," he declared to Crittenden, "Brooks and Douglas deserve statues from the Free-Soil party. The cane of the former and the Kansas Bill of the latter . . . have secured a success to the agitators. . . ."[32] The Republican state convention adopted a platform which was well designed for the situation in Massachusetts. The resolutions declared that there was no need for uniformity of opinion among the members of the party save on the question of slavery extension. The Free-Soil cause was dedicated "to God and to our Country."[33] While the Know-Nothing convention found itself divided into a Fillmore and a Frémont group, the majority favored Frémont. In general, therefore, the Frémont group was fairly well united.[34]

In New York the Democrats, since 1853, had been split into two factions, the "Hards" and the "Softs,"[35] but at the Cincinnati convention of June, 1856, the two factions reached an understanding. As a result each sent delegates to a convention which met at Syracuse July 30, and nominated a candidate for the governorship.[36]

The Fillmore following in New York was of considerable strength, mainly because many of the old Silver-Grey group, conservative men of wealth and social influence,

---

[31] The Kansas situation was the most important consideration in the Connecticut campaign. See C. L. English to Welles, New Haven, July 3, 1856, Welles MSS; *Daily Globe*, August 7, 1856. The *New York Tribune*, March 17, 1856, gives an account of the Republican state convention.

[32] Winthrop to Crittenden, July 18, 1856. Crittenden MSS.

[33] *Daily Union*, July 4, 1856.

[34] The Know-Nothings nominated Frémont and Johnson, the convention being held before the Republicans had refused to carry out the promise made by Morgan to get Dayton to withdraw in favor of Johnson. See *New York Times*, July 2, and *New York Tribune*, July 11, 1856.

[35] Johnson, *History of New York*, II, 398, 403, 406.

[36] *New York Herald*, January 11, 12; July 31, August 1, 1856.

favored the Know-Nothing ticket.[37]   The *Tribune* estimated
that Fillmore might receive a hundred thousand votes,[38]
while his followers thought he could muster two hundred
seventy thousand votes.[39]   The situation was complicated for
the Know-Nothings by the fact that there was an anti-
Fillmore Know-Nothing group headed by Hammond of the
Albany Register.[40]

As a matter of fact neither Fillmore nor Buchanan had
much chance of success after the June conventions.[41]   Many
Democratic journals came out for Frémont, and it was estimated that fifty thousand Democrats would give him their
vote.[42]   A Democratic Frémont convention was held at Syracuse in July,[43] and after that the Frémont men no longer
feared a Democratic victory.[44]   The only possible chance to
defeat Frémont in New York was the organization of a
Know-Nothing-Democratic coalition; but, while each of
these groups made common cause against Frémont, their
hostility to each other was no less marked, and there was no
real chance of a fusion movement.[45]   The energy, however,
which the Republicans put into the campaign is shown by the
fact that they spent an estimated amount of $321,000 for
campaign literature against the $59,000 which was spent by
the Democrats.[46]

However important other states may have been in the
contest of 1856, it was recognized that Pennsylvania was the
great battleground.[47]   No one knew what the result would be
in that state.   In 1854 the Whigs were able to draw to their
support the Wilmot Free-Soil group, the temperance advocates, and a considerable number of the Know-Nothings, and

---

[37] *New York Tribune,* July 11, 1856.   [38] *Ibid.*
[39] C. A. Davis to Marcey, November 16, 1856.   Marcey MSS.
[40] *Baltimore Sun,* July 2, 1856; *New York Herald,* September 18, 23, 1856.
[41] Scisco, *Political Nativism in New York,* p. 189.
[42] *Albany State Register,* quoted in *New York Herald,* March 2, 1856.
[43] Scisco, *op. cit.,* p. 183.
[44] Charles A. Dana to Pike, July 24, 1856; quoted in Pike, *First Blows of the
Civil War,* p. 345.
[45] Bryant to his brother, October 14, 1856; quoted in Goodwin, *Bryant,* II, 93.
[46] *New York Herald,* October 16, 1856.
[47] Greeley to Pike, August 6, 1856; quoted in Pike, *First Blows of the Civil
War,* p. 345; *Ohio State Journal,* July 26, 1856.

thus were able to defeat the Democrats.[48] But in the following year there was a definite break-up of the Whig organization, and the Democrats were successful in the state elections.
In March of 1856, however, the various anti-Democratic
elements of the state effected a union and placed a fusion
state ticket in the field.[49] The Democrats made no attempt
to get Know-Nothing support, openly denounced Free-
Soilism and indorsed the Kansas-Nebraska Act,[50] so that the
state election which came in October would be a definite test
of strength.

The Republicans were embarrassed by the fact that
Buchanan was a native son and supported by the most influential journals, while Frémont was not at all popular among
many Pennsylvania Whigs.[51] The Democratic appeal to the
business interests of the state, which would be damaged by
disunion, was especially potent, for it was estimated that the
South was indebted to the business men of the state to the
extent of $60,000,000.[52] The Republicans found that the
finances for the campaign expenses had to be found outside of
the state,[53] and it was patent that an unusual effort must be
put forth if the deplorable lack of enthusiasm among the
local members of their party was to be overcome.[54]

Henry B. Stanton had been selected to manage the Frémont campaign in Pennsylvania,[55] and he was supposed to
secure the aid of at least fifty public speakers.[56] As the time
for the state elections drew near, however, and it was seen
that the Republicans were not gaining ground, the chairman
of the Republican National Committee took an active part in
raising a fund of $15,000,[57] and on the eve of the election
two hundred speakers were stumping the state for the fusion

[48] Muller, *Whigs of Pennsylvania*, p. 215; *Tribune Almanac*, 1855.
[49] *Pittsburgh Post*, March 28, 1856.   [50] *New York Herald*, March 6, 1856.
[51] McClure, *Recollections*, pp. 84, 441; *Pittsburgh Post*, July 22, 1856.
[52] Muller, *Whigs of Pennsylvania*, p. 231. This was an exaggeration.
[53] Greeley to Pike, August 6, 1856; Pike, *First Blows of the Civil War*, p. 346.
[54] Charles A. Dana to Pike, October 5, 1856. *Ibid.*, p. 349.
[55] William M. Chase to Welles, July 17, 1856. Welles MSS.
[56] E. D. Morgan to Welles, July 21, 1856. Welles MSS.
[57] E. D. Morgan to Welles, September 30, October 8, 1856, Welles MSS; Russell
Everett to Chase, August 2, 1856, Chase MSS.

ticket.[58] The intensity of the campaign is well illustrated by the fact that at a great Democratic meeting at Philadelphia, September 18, there was a sufficient gathering to furnish separate audiences for eleven of the most prominent Democratic speakers.[59]

The election resulted in a Democratic victory, and, although some of the Republicans thought that the Know-Nothings had not remained true to their fusion agreement,[60] statistics show that such was not the case.[61] The election had both a local and a national significance. "I feel seriously," declared Rutherford B. Hayes, "the probable defeat of the cause of Freedom in the approaching presidential election. Before the October elections in Pennsylvania and Indiana, I was confident Colonel Frémont would be elected, but the disastrous results in those states indicate, and will probably do much to produce, his defeat. The majorities are small, very small, but they discourage our side. I shall not be surprised if Colonel Frémont receives less than one hundred electoral votes."[62] On the other hand, E. D. Morgan, the chairman of the Republican Executive Committee, began to increase his endeavors to raise funds and was still hopeful of Republican success.[63]

The Republicans realized that Buchanan would carry Pennsylvania unless they could formulate some scheme of union with the Know-Nothings. This idea had been suggested by Thurlow Weed earlier in the year but had been dropped on account of the objections raised by Greeley.[64] It

---

[58] Charles A. Dana to Pike, October 5; quoted in Pike, *op. cit.*, p. 349.

[59] These speakers were gathered from ten different states. See *Daily Union*, September 20, 1856.

[60] William M. Chase to Welles, October 21, 1856. Welles MSS. Others thought that the Democrats had purchased foreign votes. See McClure, *Notes on Pennsylvania*, I, 258; also *New York Herald*, October 17, 1856.

[61] In the presidential election the combined fusion and Fillmore vote was 1,025 less than the Democratic. See *Tribune Almanac*, 1857, p. 48.

[62] Williams (Ed.), *Diary and Letters of Rutherford B. Hayes*, I, 502; the *New York Herald* practically conceded the election to Buchanan after the October elections. See issue of October 19, 1856.

[63] E. D. Morgan to Welles, October 22, 1856. Welles MSS.

[64] Charles A. Dana to Pike, July 24, 1856; quoted in Pike, *First Blows of the Civil War*, p. 345.

was taken up again, however, and Francis P. Blair, together with Simon Cameron, Thurlow Weed, and Henry Wilson, developed the plan of a union electoral ticket.[65] The Fillmore men lacked enthusiasm for the scheme, and at a meeting of their state committee the majority were in the opposition.[66] Various proposals of co-operation were rejected by the Know-Nothings,[67] until finally a minority of their state committee acted with the Republicans in arranging a scheme whereby a joint ticket of twenty-seven electors was chosen, twenty-six of whom should be voted for by both parties. In the event of their election, their vote would be divided between the parties in accordance with the number of votes given by each party to its twenty-seventh elector.[68] Of course those of the Know-Nothings who did not approve of this scheme continued to support Fillmore.

After this arrangement was made the Republicans redoubled their efforts to carry the state. Chase, Cameron, Truman Smith, and others from various parts of the country went to Pennsylvania to do what they could to stem the tide.[69] They delivered speeches and were authorized to dispense funds "wherever they deem it most judicious," the supply being in excess of $25,000.[70]

In the November election Buchanan carried the state by a large plurality and a small clear majority of all votes cast. Several counties of the state, such as Dauphin, Chester, Delaware, and Lancaster, which were Whig in 1852 and Fusion in the October election of 1856 but which were carried by Buchanan in November, polled a Fillmore vote of sufficient strength to have changed the election result had it been given to Frémont. Furthermore, some counties which were nominally Democratic but in 1856 polled a negligible Fillmore vote, were carried by Frémont. This would seem to indicate

---

[65] E. D. Morgan to Welles, October 15, 1856, Welles MSS; McClure, *Recollections,* p. 45.

[66] R. P. Letcher to Crittenden, October 20, 1856. Crittenden MSS.

[67] E. D. Morgan to Welles, October 18, 1856. Welles MSS.

[68] Muller, *Whig Party in Pennsylvania,* p. 235; McClure, *Notes on Pennsylvania,* I, 259.

[69] E. D. Morgan to Welles, October 27, 1856. Welles MSS.   [70] *Ibid.*

that the vote given to Fillmore was disastrous to the Frémont cause.[71] Yet the situation in these counties is sufficiently
exceptional to exclude the possibility of a generalization, and,
at any rate, there is no available evidence to indicate that
those men who voted for the conservative candidate, Fillmore, would have voted against the conservative candidate,
Buchanan.[72] It may be noted in passing that this statement
in regard to the importance of the candidacy of Fillmore is
equally true in regard to Illinois, substantiated by the
example of Indiana, and in fact applies to the whole Northwest as well as to Pennsylvania.[73]

During the campaign Frémont remained at his home in
New York, where he received numerous visitors and delegations.[74] Ordinarily he delivered a short address to his
visitors, but without committing himself on political questions. Thus, to a delegation of booksellers, he declared that
the political contest was a great movement of the people to
regenerate the government.[75] To some extent he made the
office of John Howard, his financial agent, his personal headquarters during the campaign.[76]

Frémont possessed elements both of strength and of
weakness as a candidate. His charm of manner, magnetism
of personality, and dignity of bearing enabled him to make
many friends.[77] Stories of his deeds of heroism as an explorer
filled the pages of several campaign biographies and may
have appealed to some people throughout the land.[78] The
word "Frémont" lent itself easily to alliteration with "free-
speech," "free-soil," and the like, and a book of songs about
"Frémont and Jessie" was published. Charles A. Dana

---

[71] These facts are taken from election returns as reported in *Tribune Almanac*,
1857.
[72] Greeley thought that the Fillmore candidacy caused Frémont's defeat. See
Greeley, *Recollections*, p.. 354.
[73] See Buley, "The Political Balance in the Old Northwest," *Indiana Studies in
American History*, 1926, p. 449.
[74] *New York Herald*, October 25, 1856.
[75] *Ibid.*, September 19, 1856.
[76] Howard, *Reminiscences*, p. 37.
[77] Martin, *Life of Choate*, p. 197; Rothschild, *Lincoln*, p. 294.
[78] Elizabeth Whittier said he had been her hero for years. See Smith, *Political
History of Slavery*, I, 230; Greeley, *Recollections*, p. 354.

became more and more enthusiastic about him as a campaign figure, and the *New York Times* thought that no party had ever had such an excellent candidate.[79] A good contemporary estimate of his candidacy was written by Rutherford B. Hayes soon after the election. "But he did make," said Hayes, "a fine run and has borne himself admirably through the trying canvass which is closed. He may not become a permanent figure among the leading men, but I think he is so likely to do so that I shall now buy his portrait to put in my parlor."[80]

On the other hand, it was thought that Frémont, if elected, would be dominated by such men as Blair, Greeley, and Weed.[81] Democratic journals could point out that mountain-climbing did not prepare a man to understand correctly the Constitution; and tactful Democratic speakers, though praising Frémont as an explorer, showed that such service did not fit him for the conduct of foreign relations which required the skill and prudence of a person long trained in public service.[82]

The contest of 1856 was not without personal incriminations which so often abound in political struggles, and which, though trivial in themselves, are of moment in the campaign. Frémont had participated in several encounters which, though settled without bloodshed, furnished materials that could be used by the Democrats to counteract the influence of the Brooks-Sumner affair.[83] Then certain of Frémont's acts while he was military governor of California were recounted by his opponents in such a way as to make it appear that he was dishonest.[84] The most influential attack on Fré-

---

[79] November 6, 1856. That was soon after the election.

[80] Hayes to S. Birchard, November 16, 1856, in Williams, *Hayes' Diary*, I, 504.

[81] Martin Van Buren to Tilden, September 1, 1856, in Bigelow, *Tilden*, I, 119

[82] See Speech of John Dickinson at Birmingham, New York, June 21, quoted in *Dickinson's Speeches*, I, 508-24.

[83] Bigelow included these stories in his *Life of Frémont* against the advice of the latter. See Dana to Pike, August 9, 1856, in Pike, *First Blows of the Civil War*, p. 347. See also the story of his affair with Foote, Foote, *The War of the Rebellion*, p. 211; also *New York Tribune*, October 15, 1856.

[84] See *New York Tribune*, September 9, 1856, for a defense of Frémont, and *Pittsburgh Post*, July 29, 1856, for accusation.

mont, however, was the charge that he was a Catholic.   Several facts about his life, such as his French origin, his education at a Catholic school, and his marriage by a Catholic minister, gave some circumstantial evidence that he was a Catholic.   At any rate, the charge was made and persisted during the entire campaign.   The caricatures of the period presented Frémont promising that Catholics would be favored were he elected.[85]   Seward declared that Frémont was "nearly convicted of being a Catholic,"[86] and the Republican press was constantly on the defensive to disprove the charge.[87]   Delegations visited him and later made public statements to the effect that they were authorized to report that he was a Protestant,[88] and the records of the baptism of his children and their admission into Protestant churches were made public.[89]

Schuyler Colfax declared that scarcely one of the hundreds of letters which he received from the Northwest omitted "a reference to the fact that the Catholic story" injured Frémont materially, and that Frémont's silence on the subject was largely responsible for the continuance of rumors about it.[90]   On the eve of the election it was stated that if Frémont lost the election it would be on account of the belief which prevailed among many people that he was a Catholic.[91]   Frémont maintained a complete silence on the subject, an attitude later explained by his daughter on the ground that while he had always been a Protestant, he refused to discuss his religion because it would be a tacit admission that such a matter was of political importance.[92]

Some of Frémont's followers were so certain of his election that they began to discuss the personnel of his coming

---

[85] An extraordinarily fine collection of these is to be found at the Ridgeway Branch of the Philadelphia Public Library.

[86] Seward to his Family, August 17, 1856, quoted in Seward, *Seward at Washington*, II, 287.

[87] *Daily News*, September 26, 1856; *New York Herald*, October 28, 1856; *New York Tribune*, October 10, 1856.

[88] *Daily News*, September 26, 1856.   [89] *Ibid.*

[90] Colfax to Bigelow, August 29, 1856.   Bigelow MSS (New York Pub. Lib.).

[91] *Washington Evening Star*, November 3, 1856.

[92] Elizabeth Frémont, *Recollections*.

administration,[93] while others declared that they had foreseen his defeat.[94] The Republican failure was accounted for in various ways. Some people thought the Fillmore candidacy was responsible;[95] others that Frémont was weak as a candidate;[96] others that the foreign-born Irish and Germans had turned the tide;[97] and others laid the blame on the alleged fraud and corruption of the Democrats.[98] More conservative men, however, were inclined to view the campaign as a Republican victory, in that a strong political organization had been created and the foundation had been laid for a successful campaign in 1860.[99]

---

[93] Dana to Pike, August 9, 1856, quoted in Pike, *First Blows of the Civil War*, p. 347; T. Ruffin to Ruffin, Hamilton, *Ruffin Papers*, II, 518.

[94] H. Forbes to Chase, November 5, 1856. Chase MSS.

[95] Greeley, *Recollections*, p. 354.

[96] G. F. Talbott to Washburn, November 16, 1856. Israel Washburn MSS.

[97] *Philadelphia Daily News*, November 10, 1856; *New York Times*, November 6, 1856.

[98] Forney, *Anecdotes of Public Men*, II, 240.

[99] E. D. Morgan to Welles, November 6, 1856, Welles MSS; *New York Times*, November 5, 1856.

CHAPTER VI

FRÉMONT IN MISSOURI

For a time after the campaign of 1856, Frémont turned his attention to the development of his California estate,[1] although he spent a part of his time in New York and kept in touch with political affairs.[2] In 1860 he was considered as one of the possible Republican candidates for the presidency,[3] but no considerable following developed. The Blairs no longer supported him for that office, Montgomery Blair being quoted as saying that the country had made a fortunate escape in 1856,[4] and Preston King and Gideon Welles were turned aside from their attempt to support him through the influence of John Bigelow.[5] It is not surprising, then, that he received but a few scattering votes at the Republican nominating convention.

Frémont remained, however, a political factor and was prominently mentioned as a probable cabinet officer in the new administration.[6] President-elect Lincoln, without advice from anyone, decided to provide for Frémont by giving him the ambassadorship to France. William L. Dayton was to have the corresponding position at the Court of St. James.[7] This plan was upset by Seward, who as the future Secretary of State insisted that Charles Francis Adams should be sent to England and Dayton to France.[8] Seward suggested that Frémont should be made Secretary of War, but Cameron

---

[1] For the story of Frémont's estate in California, see Browne, *Mariposa*.
[2] Jessie B. Frémont to F. P. Blair, Jr., February 25, 1858. Frémont MSS.
[3] Spooner to Welles, March 3, 1860, Welles MSS; *New York Tribune*, February 28, 1860.
[4] Preston King to Welles, March 3, and March 31, 1860. Welles MSS.
[5] *Ibid.*, Bigelow circulated a rumor concerning Frémont's moral character.
[6] Ward to Chase, February 11, 1861. Chase MSS.
[7] C. F. Adams, *Life of C. F. Adams*, p. 144; Rothschild, *Lincoln*, p. 292; Nicolay and Hay, *Lincoln*, IV, 402.
[8] *Ibid.*

had to be provided for, and, since that place fell to him, Frémont was left out altogether.[9]

When the War broke out Frémont was in Paris, but almost immediately there was a popular demand that he should be appointed to a responsible position in the Northern armies, and it was suggested that he should receive a western post.[10] Governor Yates of Illinois and other people of the west urged Gustave Koerner to make a special trip to see the President and to suggest such an appointment.[11] He was mentioned in extravagant terms of praise at Washington,[12] and Secretary Chase suggested that he should be placed in command of the Shenandoah Valley,[13] although the regular army men did not look with favor on his appointment at all.[14] There is no doubt, however, that the Blairs influenced the President considerably, not only in the decision to place him in high command, but also in the determination to give him a western post. Frémont, therefore, was given a major generalship on the same day that George B. McClellan was given a like commission; and the Western Department was created three days later.[15]

The situation in Missouri was one of great confusion. Without doubt the majority of the people of Missouri wished to preserve a position of neutrality similar to that which the central government permitted to exist in Kentucky.[16] Unfortunately that desire was frustrated. The radical politician, Francis P. Blair, Jr., aided by the fanatical Captain Nathaniel Lyon, fanned the sparks of discord into a flame and brought about a condition of active civil war within that state.[17]

[9] Nicolay and Hay, *Lincoln*, III, 362.

[10] *New York Tribune*, May 15, 30, 1861.

[11] Koerner, *Memoirs*, II, 152.

[12] Schurz, *Reminiscences*, II, 341.

[13] Chase to Frémont, August 4, 1861, quoted in *New York Tribune*, March 17, 1862.

[14] Frémont to Mrs. Frémont, October 12, 1861; quoted in Jessie B. Frémont, *Chronicle of the Guard*, p. 86.

[15] July 3, 1861, *Official Records*, III, 390.

[16] A good brief account of the situation in Missouri may be found in Smith, *The Borderland in the Civil War*.

[17] For further insight into Missouri affairs the student should consult Laughlin, *Missouri Politics in the Civil War*.

When Frémont arrived in St. Louis, Captain Lyon with a small body of troops was occupying a precarious position in the southwestern part of the state, while the Confederate forces were threatening an invasion from the southeast; the whole state was rife with rebellion. Frémont decided that it was more expedient and of greater value to the Union cause to protect posts along the Mississippi River than to hold the southwestern part of the state. His immediate efforts, therefore, were directed toward the strengthening of Cairo, and, although some aid was sent to Captain Lyon, the situation was such that it was of but little assistance.

The critics of Frémont[18] have maintained that he not only made an error of judgment in deciding that Cairo was the true strategic point of defense, but that he could have exerted greater efforts to relieve General Lyon. In view of the evidence taken by the Committee on the Conduct of the War, there can be but little doubt that to strengthen Cairo and other points in that area was not an error of strategy. As for Lyon, there was a clear line of procedure open for him. He had decided on August 4 that he was under the "painful necessity of retreating" and that he could hope only to make his retreat good.[19] The road to Rolla, Missouri, where there were supplies and equipment, was open; he had ample transportation, and if there were valuable supplies and equipment in his camp, they could have been sent safely ahead. His officers advised him to withdraw,[20] and it was generally supposed, at Frémont's headquarters, that he would do so until he was reinforced sufficiently to make a stand.[21] He decided, however, to attack and formed a plan of action with the advice of but one of his generals, Siegel, who did not play a brilliant part in the sub-

---

[18] Contemporary critics such as General Thomas and Francis P. Blair, Jr., and recent critics such as James Ford Rhodes and biographers of Lyon. See report of Thomas to the Secretary of War, *Official Records*, III, 540; Rhodes, *History of the United States*, III, 468; Woodward, *Life of Lyon.*

[19] *Official Records*, III, 48.

[20] Testimony of General Sturgis, second in command, *Report of Committee on Conduct of the War*, III, 225.

[21] Testimony of Colonel I. C. Woods stationed at St. Louis, *Ibid.*, p. 204.

sequent engagement. The battle, known as that of Wilson's Creek, took place on August 10; and, according to General Schofield, Lyon realized that the battle was lost before it was half over and threw away his life by needless exposure.[22]

The Confederates did not immediately follow up their advantage gained by their victory at Wilson's Creek. Frémont occupied his time in gathering, equipping, and training an army, and in making general military preparations. It was not until the beginning of September that the Confederate General Price moved his army northward from Springfield and into the vicinity of Lexington on the Missouri River.[23] The Northern forces in that area were under the command of Colonel James A. Mulligan, who retreated to Lexington, where he was besieged by Price. A series of circumstances, including the lack of military skill and foresight on the part of Colonel Mulligan, and lack of energy on the part of General Pope, caused Lexington and the forces under Mulligan to fall into the hands of the Confederates.[24] Owing to the peculiar situation that developed regarding Frémont's position in Missouri, the affairs of Wilson's Creek and Lexington received notoriety far in excess of their real importance.

Not the least of the difficulties that any Northern commander had to face in Missouri was the fact that the majority of Missourians were not in sympathy with the attempt of the North to coerce the South. In 1862, General W. T. Sherman defended the conduct of Frémont's successor, General Halleck, on the ground that the "politicians" considered only the number of troops engaged in the west and not the fact that the country was overrun with secessionists.[25] Frémont was obliged to keep small bands of troops at many places throughout the state merely to preserve order.[26] He

[22] Schofield, Forty-six Years in the Army, p. 42.
[23] There had been conflict between Confederate leaders as to a plan of action.
[24] This affair may be studied in the Official Records, III, and in the Report of the Committee on the Conduct of the War, III.
[25] W. T. Sherman to Senator Sherman, January 7, 1862, in Thorndyke, Sherman Letters, p. 138. Sherman was in Missouri.
[26] Snead, "First Year of the War in Missouri," Battles and Leaders, I, 274.

decided to combat that situation by the use of martial law and the threat of property confiscation. Accordingly, he proclaimed that he would confiscate the property and free the slaves of all persons within his department who took up arms against the Union or assisted in the field the enemies of the same.[27]   President Lincoln requested Frémont to modify the slavery provision of the proclamation, saying that the "Southern-union friends" of the government might take alarm at such a measure.[28]   When Frémont refused to modify the order on his own initiative,[29] the President officially ordered him to so do,[30] and discovered a legal, as well as a political reason for his act.   In a long letter to a political friend he explained that Frémont's action was "purely political" and not within the range of "military law or necessity."   He denied that a military commander could fix the permanent future status of property.   "Can it be pretended," he said, "that it is any longer the Government of the United States—any government of constitution and laws—wherein a general or a president may make permanent rules of property by proclamation?   I do not say that Congress might not with propriety pass a law on the point, just as General Frémont proclaimed.   I do not say I might not, as a member of Congress, vote for it.   What I object to is, that I, as President, shall expressly or impliedly seize and exercise the permanent legislative functions of the government."[31]

President Lincoln's act of modification caused scarcely less commotion in the country than Frémont's proclamation. Some of the most important Republican journals expressed their disagreement with the President.[32]   The *New York Tribune* defended Frémont as to his right and power to confiscate slave property, but apologized for the President's

---

[27] *Official Records*, III, 467.   Rhodes and Nicolay and Hay do not prove their statements that Frémont had other reasons.
[28] *Official Records*, III, 469.
[29] *Ibid.*, p. 477.
[30] *Ibid.*, p. 485.
[31] Lincoln to Browning, Sept. 22, 1861; quoted in Stevens, *Lincoln in Missouri*, p. 79.
[32] Cole, "President Lincoln and His War-Time Critics," *History Teachers Magazine*, 1918, p. 245.

course on the grounds that he differed from Frémont as to the necessity for the act.[33] "The President's letter to General Frémont," declared John Medill of the *Chicago Tribune,* "has caused a funereal gloom over our patriotic city. We are stricken with a heavier calamity than the battle of Bull Run. It comes upon us like a killing June frost, which destroys the coming harvest. It is a *step backwards,* and *backward* steps seldom lead to good results."[34] Medill did not hesitate to voice in his paper the same sentiments that he expressed in private correspondence.[35]

The majority of the Republicans of Illinois gave their support to Frémont.[36] One writer declared that Lincoln's policy had given more "aid and comfort" to the enemy in Missouri than a present of fifty pieces of cannon.[37] The *National Anti-Slavery Standard* thought that Lincoln had committed a blunder worse than crime in yielding to border-state proslavery influence,[38] and the *Liberator* hailed Frémont's order as the most satisfactory event that had happened since the war.[39] Harriet Beecher Stowe believed that "the hour had come and the man."[40] The *Ohio State Journal* stated that scarcely a paper favoring a vigorous prosecution of the war objected to Frémont's proclamation;[41] while Judge Brinkerhof of Cincinnati recorded that the President's policy fell "like lead upon the hearts of the people of Ohio."[42]

The whole controversy over Frémont's slavery proclamation soon became involved with his unfortunate controversy with the Blairs.[43] When Frémont went to Missouri, Francis P. Blair, Jr., went along to see that he got properly

---

[33] September 16, 1861.
[34] Medill to Chase, September 15, 1861. Chase MSS.
[35] *Chicago Tribune,* September 16, 1861.
[36] Cole, *Era of the Civil War,* p. 292.
[37] Russell to Trumbull, December 17, 1861. Trumbull MSS.
[38] September 28, 1861.
[39] September 20, 1861.
[40] *Liberator,* September 20, 1861.
[41] September 20, 1861.
[42] Brinkerhof to Chase, September, 1861. Chase MSS.
[43] Laughlin, *Missouri Politics,* p. 99.

started, and for a time the relations between them were cordial.[44] The Blairs thought that Frémont would follow their advice on matters of importance. In fact, that seems to be the reason why they urged his appointment to the command of the Western Department. For a time their influence was considerable; several staff appointments were made at their suggestion, and the younger Blair was influential at headquarters.[45] About the middle of August the personal relations between Frémont and the younger Blair became less cordial, and by the end of the month the latter was in open hostility.[46] The hostility of Francis, Jr., was immediately adopted by the rest of the family.[47]

One of the members of Frémont's staff later declared that Francis P. Blair, Jr., who was in nominal command of a regiment under Frémont, attempted to dictate to him, and, failing in that, determined to ruin his administration and get him removed.[48] At any rate Frémont did not seek advice from Blair very frequently, and it is significant that the latter wrote to his brother, Montgomery Blair, in condemnation of Frémont only a few days after Frémont had refused to award a large army contract to Blair's friends in spite of Blair's specific request that he should do so.[49] Blair represented that Frémont lacked vigor; that discipline in his army was bad; that he did not take advice; that he had not sent the proper military support to General Lyon; in short, that he should be removed.[50]

If Francis P. Blair counted on the influence that his brother might be able to exert upon the President he was not disappointed, for the Postmaster-General, playing his rôle very adroitly, showed the President his letters from his brother, at the same time assuming an attitude of deep regret

[44] Stevens, *Lincoln and Missouri*, p. 77.
[45] Testimony of Blair, *Committee on Conduct of the War, Report*, III, 155.
[46] Schofield, *Forty-six Years in the Army*, p. 49.
[47] Testimony of Montgomery Blair, *Committee on Conduct of the War*, III, 155.
[48] Howard, *Reminiscences*, p. 149.
[49] Testimony of F. P. Blair, Jr., *Committee on Conduct of the War*, III, 179.
[50] F. P. Blair to Montgomery Blair, September 1, 1861; quoted in *New York Tribune*, October 7, 1861.

that Frémont had not fulfilled expectations.[51] The President was convinced of the truth of the story of the Blairs but not ready to remove Frémont. Instead, he sent General Hunter to Missouri to assist in the management of affairs there. He told Hunter that Frémont isolated himself, and that he was losing the confidence of men of importance.[52]

The President's belief that Frémont's greatest mistake was his exclusiveness shows that he relied upon the Blairs for his information.[53] It is an unusually noteworthy charge, for it is one of those made against Frémont that had no adequate foundation.[54] The widespread criticism of Frémont that began to appear in the press was remarkably similar also to the allegations made by the Blairs and shows the same lack of evidence. The *New York Times* may be taken as an example. More editorial space was given to the fall of Lexington than to the battle of Bull Run. "Think of it," declared the editor, "this army just struck out of existence was nearly as numerous as that with which the brave Lyon encountered Ben McCulloch. . . . The loss of Lexington is a gigantic crime, we care not at whose door it lies."[55] More comment followed but no real account of the facts was printed.

The President was inclined to consider that the reports which came from the west were sent out by people who were profiting from army contracts made with Frémont.[56] He decided to send the Secretary of War to visit the Western Department with discretionary power to remove Frémont and to make a report on the situation.[57] The Secretary took along with him Adjutant General Thomas, who also was to make a report. The Adjutant General was not an impartial

---

[51] Montgomery Blair may have been no better informed than Lincoln.

[52] Nicolay and Hay, *Lincoln*, IV, 413.

[53] This statement was made about the time that he saw the letter from Francis Blair, Jr.

[54] *Committee on Conduct of the War, Report*, III, 205; report of Thomas, *Official Records*, III, 540 ff; letter of Colfax to *New York Tribune*, September 28, 1861; Howard, *Reminiscences*, p. 144.

[55] *New York Times*, September 25, 1861.

[56] B. R. Ploomly to Chase, October 19, 1861. Chase MSS.

[57] Nicolay and Hay, *Lincoln*, IV, 430.

investigator, because he had already expressed the opinion that "everything in the West, military and financial, was in confusion."[58]   The competence of Secretary Cameron to judge the ability of military men is demonstrated by the fact that after a visit to General W. T. Sherman he was convinced that the General was "absolutely crazy."[59]   The report that was made by the Adjutant General is one of the most enlightening documents connected with the whole Frémont affair.[60]   It was a combination of statements made by some of Frémont's generals, rumors that were current, and personal observations and opinions.   It contained the opinion of General Curtis, who was already known to be hostile to Frémont,[61] and that of General Hunter, who, in addition to being the probable successor to Frémont if he were removed, had already written letters against him.[62]   Four other commanders of divisions were not interviewed.   Thomas reported the curious and unauthenticated story told to him by General Sherman, to the effect that Colonel Swords had reported that Major Selover had written to a friend that he had made a huge profit out of a contract for guns which he had purchased for Frémont.

This report of the Adjutant General was immediately given to the press and made public—a fact which was scarcely less noteworthy than the report itself.   It is difficult to explain the whole matter of the Thomas report on any other ground than a desire on the part of the Government to prepare the public for Frémont's removal.   The obvious superficiality of the investigation, the *ex parte* nature of the testimony, and the strained attempt to discover incompetence in Frémont's Department was noted at the time.[63]   The *New York Times* spoke of the report as the "diary of a travelling Adjutant," which was the most remarkable document since the beginning of the war.[64]   It is significant that, at the time

---

[58] Nicolay, *Personal Traits*, pp. 178-79.
[59] Conversation with Cameron, McClure, *Recollections*, p. 332.
[60] *Official Records*, III, 540-49.   [62] Nicolay and Hay, *Lincoln*, IV, 432.
[61] *Ibid.*, p. 541.   [63] *New York Tribune*, October 30, 1861.
[64] October 31, 1861; *Missouri Democrat*, November 8, 1861, gives a good summary of press comment.

when General Thomas was criticizing the construction of fortifications about St. Louis as being unnecessary and ordering the work to be stopped, General Sherman was writing that there was danger of that city's being attacked, and that its loss would be more disastrous than the capture of Washington.[65] General Price, whom Frémont was then trying to overtake, was urging the Confederacy to attack St. Louis while Frémont was away.[66]

In the meantime other irons were in the fire. The House of Representatives, July 8, had appointed a committee to investigate war contracts.[67] This committee was originally intended to consider the conduct of the Secretary of War,[68] but for some reason it was induced to turn its attention for a time to the Western Department. The report was not given until December 17, but during the controversy mentioned above members of that committee were securing testimony about army contracts in the west and writing letters about what the committee would make known when the report was ready. Thus Elihu B. Washburn of Illinois informed Chase that the way in which money was expended at St. Louis would "astound the world and disgrace . . . a nation."[69] "Such robbery," he said, "fraud, extravagance, speculation, as have been developed in Frémont's department can hardly be conceived of. There has been an organized system of pillage right under the eye of Frémont."

Montgomery Blair was not idle during the time the fate of Frémont was in the balance. To the Secretary of the Treasury he represented that Frémont was doing nothing to repel the Confederate invasion in Missouri, while he was surrounded by speculators who were reported to be connected with Jewish firms in New York, which fact alone was enough to injure the credit of the Government.[70] He attempted to

---

[65] General Sherman to Senator Sherman, October 5, 1861; quoted in Thorndyke, *The Sherman Letters*, p. 132.
[66] General Price to A. S. Johnson, November 7, 1861. *Official Records*, III, 731.
[67] 37th Cong., 1st Sess., *Globe*, p. 23.
[68] Grimes to Mrs. Grimes, November 13, 1861; quoted in Salter, *Life of Grimes*, p. 154. [69] Cairo, Illinois, October 31, 1861. Chase MSS.
[70] Montgomery Blair to Chase, October 16, 1861. Chase MSS (Pa. Hist. Soc.).

impress Chase with the idea that Frémont was treating the administration with contempt. "The danger," he said, "is that solid sensible men, seeing that the administration submits to the insults of such an imbecile jackass will come to think we are getting only our deserts because we submit to such treatment. This will injure our credit and perhaps has affected it."[71] While he thus made one sort of an appeal to Secretary Chase, he was busy making statements elsewhere. To Governor Andrew of Massachusetts a long epistolary attack on Frémont was made. The "Brave Lyon," the "loss of Lexington," the exclusiveness of Frémont, and all the other points were mentioned. The heroic efforts of Francis P. Blair, and other points were duly noted. In the end, Governor Andrew was requested to do what he could for the removal of Frémont.[72] Francis P. Blair, Sr., was also busy writing letters from Silver Spring to former friends of Frémont, charging him with maladministration, incompetence, and disobedience of the orders of the President.[73]

President Lincoln had decided three times to remove Frémont, but had hesitated, apparently because the Secretary of State, Seward, had not favored such a move.[74] Soon after the publication of the Thomas report, however, a Cabinet meeting was held,[75] and on October 24, President Lincoln wrote the order for his removal. It was specified that the order should not be delivered if in the meantime Frémont won a victory, or if at the time the order reached his camp he were on the eve of battle.[76] The winning of a battle was out of the question because the Confederate General Price had rapidly retreated before Frémont. The latter had attempted to cut off the retreat of Price and force a battle, but he was hindered somewhat in his advance by lack of good transportation, by the confusion occasioned by the constant rumors of

[71] *Ibid.*
[72] Montgomery Blair to Andrew, October 2, 1861. Andrew MSS.
[73] Blair to Bigelow, October 26, 1861; quoted in Bigelow, *Retrospections*, I, 376.
[74] *Ibid.* This is the story as Blair told it.
[75] *New York Tribune*, October 23, 24, contains news from Washington about Cabinet meeting to discuss Frémont.
[76] *Official Records*, III, 553.

his removal, and by the lack of co-operation on the part of Generals Pope and Hunter.[77] Consequently the order for his removal was handed to him on November 2, and General Hunter succeeded him.[78]

General Frémont was mistaken in his belief that he was removed on the eve of battle, for General Price had no intention of making a stand.[79] Frémont had succeeded in advancing as far as Springfield, only three months after Lyon had lost it; but, when he was relieved by Hunter, the latter promptly abandoned that part of the state, which was thought to have been so important when Lyon attempted to hold it.[80]

Various solutions were offered to explain the removal of Frémont. Schuyler Colfax believed that the controversy with the Blairs was the primary reason, the Blairs having sufficient influence to accomplish his removal.[81] Grimes was thoroughly convinced that the slavery proclamation was the real cause.[82] He believed that there had been an organized conspiracy against him, which conviction was proven by the fact that the officers were sent to spy upon him;[83] by the conduct of the House Committee on Contracts, which was composed of enemies; by the stimulation given to subordinate generals to disobey his orders; and by the repetition of false rumors concerning his removal.[84] Whatever may have been the force of these various things, it is certain that the charges against Frémont, of corruption and extravagances and of military incapacity, were large factors in his removal. The report of the House Committee on Contracts, which found great fault with Frémont's régime, was uncritical, subject to contradiction, and evidently partisan.[85] Corruption

---

[77] Howard, *Reminiscences*, pp. 157-68.

[78] *Official Records*, III, 559.   [79] *Ibid.*, p. 731.

[80] *Report of Committee on Conduct of the War*, III, 5.

[81] Hollister, *Colfax*, p. 181.

[82] Grimes to Fessenden, November 13, 1861; quoted in Salter, *Grimes*, p. 155.

[83] He probably meant General Hunter.

[84] See Grimes to Fessenden, November 13, *op. cit.*; he might have included the Thomas Report.

[85] *Committee on Contracts, House Report*, 37th Cong., 2nd Sess., No. 1. Critical study reveals definite proof of this statement.

in contracts given out by Frémont did not involve Frémont personally and could have been remedied without Frémont's removal. The President made Frémont's continuance in command depend upon a military victory, which Frémont was unable to accomplish on a moment's notice. He freed the area under his command from guerrilla bands, secured the important river posts, and whether he would have been successful in leading an army to Memphis and beyond could hardly have been foreseen in 1861.[86]

When Frémont left Missouri he went to New York and, in January, 1862, appeared before the Committee on Conduct of the War. His defense before the Committee and the favorable character of their report concerning him, together with the opposition raised in Congress to the report of the Committee, tended to strengthen the popular feeling that Frémont had been unjustly removed from command.[87] At any rate, by February 1, 1862, the Government had decided to give Frémont a new command.[88] The press began to report that such would be the case,[89] and it was rumored that he would be sent to Texas.

The President, however, had other plans. He was interested in the Northern sentiment which had developed in eastern Tennessee and in making an attempt to secure that area for the North.[90] Also there was a considerable body of unoccupied troops stationed at Wheeling, West Virginia. It was decided to create a new military area, the Mountain Department, which should include the territory between the departments of the Potomac and the Mississippi, and separated from the latter by a line drawn north and south through Knoxville.[91] Frémont was given command of this area, and his duty was to guard the railroads, put down guerrilla bands,

---

[86] At the time he was removed, the situation of the Confederacy was favorable for a Union expedition. The Confederates were surprised to learn that General Hunter returned from Springfield with the Union army. See R. W. Johnston to A. S. Johnston, November 18, 1861, *Official Records*, IV, 562.

[87] Dana, *Recollections*, p. 5; Conway, *Reminiscences*, I, 380.

[88] Stanton to Dana, February 1, 1862; quoted in Dana, *Recollections*, p. 6.

[89] *New York Tribune*, February 14, 1862.

[90] *Official Records*, V, 54.

[91] *Ibid.*

and, as soon as he had been reinforced, to move toward Knoxville.[92]

The story of Frémont's experiences as commander of the Mountain Department is again one of adversity. He was directed to assist in the frantic attempt to cut off the retreat of General Jackson from the Shenandoah Valley, but for one reason or another was not successful.[93]

The administration realized that the multiplicity of commanding generals with independent forces within the same area was inexpedient, and on June 26 General Pope was placed in charge of the combined forces. Frémont was unwilling to accept a subordinate position under General Pope, since that officer had so ardently opposed him in Missouri. He requested, therefore, an interview with the Secretary of War,[94] and, on being refused, asked to be relieved from command.[95]

Frémont entertained hopes that he would receive a new command,[96] and influential friends besought the President in his behalf; but he remained on the inactive list until 1864, when he resigned from the army.

[92] Frémont's Report, *Official Records*, XII, Pt. 1, p. 7.

[93] For this story the best references are: Jacob B. Cox, "West Virginia Under Frémont," *Battles and Leaders*, II, 279 ff.; Allan, *Jackson in the Shenandoah*; and *Official Records*, XII, Pt. 1.

[94] Howard, *Reminiscences*, p. 189. Howard was sent to ask for the interview.

[95] *Official Records*, XII, Pt. 3, p. 438.

[96] Frémont to Andrew, July 5, 1862. Andrew MSS.

CHAPTER VII

THE GROWTH OF A RADICAL PARTY
1861-1864

From the time that President Lincoln modified the slavery proclamation of General Frémont, there was a growing rift in the Republican party, occasioned by the difference of opinion on the slavery question.[1] "In fact," said the *Cincinnati Gazette*, "we should be suppressing the truth to no good purpose if we should refrain from saying that the course in modifying General Frémont's proclamation, so as to exempt the property of rebels in arms from the penalties of rebellion, has greatly damaged the administration in the estimation of the people, without distinction of party."[2] A considerable group of Republicans began to feel that the President was not sufficiently hostile to the institution of slavery, and this group, known as radical Republicans, was not without political leadership. Senator Grimes of Iowa voiced the anti-slavery sentiment of his state.[3] In Indiana Governor Oliver P. Morton and G. W. Julian represented a similar opinion,[4] and in Illinois John Wentworth of the *Chicago Tribune* and Senator Trumbull found themselves out of sympathy with the President.[5] In New York the opposition to the administration was sufficient to convince John Jay that an uprising might take place,[6] and it was reported that many people of that state thought that the President should resign because he was "fickle, careless, and totally unqualified" to lead the

---

[1] See Cole, "President Lincoln and Illinois Radical Republicans," *Mississippi Valley Historical Review*, IV, 420 ff.; Cole, "President Lincoln and his War-Time Critics," *History Teachers' Magazine*, May 1918, pp. 248 ff.
[2] *Cincinnati Gazette*, September 24, 1861.
[3] Grimes to Chase, July 29, 1862. Chase MSS.
[4] Woodburn, "Indiana," *American Historical Association Report*, I, 228 (1902).
[5] Cole, "President Lincoln and his War-Time Critics," *op. cit.*, p. 421.
[6] John Jay to Chase, September 27, 1862. Chase MSS.

Government.[7] "The simple truth," said William P. Fessenden, "is that never was such a shambling half-and-half set of incapables collected in one government before since the world began." He believed that the King of Siam had more understanding of the situation in the North than the President had.[8] At another occasion he wrote: "I am at times almost in despair. Well, it cannot be helped. We went in for a rail-splitter, and we have got one." These were the private thoughts of Fessenden. Publicly he supported Lincoln because he thought it politically expedient.[9]

In the elections of 1862, the Republicans lost control of six Northern states. Of course the amount of direct influence on the election of the administration's treatment of Frémont is problematical, but the comment of the press in condemning the administration for its acts in that regard could not have been without effect; at any rate, after the elections of that year the opposition to the President took a more decided turn.

There were a number of public men who thought that Lincoln was surrounded by a group of advisers who exercised a harmful influence upon him, and that the chief of these was Seward.[10] In response to that belief a series of senatorial meetings was held to petition the President to remove his chief secretary. In this series of meetings the Senators expressed their opinions freely. Senator Wilkinson thought the country was lost, and that Seward should be removed from the Cabinet. Senators Grimes, Wade, Collamer, and others spoke to the same purpose, while Senator Sherman, of Ohio, believed that the President, who lacked "dignity, order, or firmness," was to blame. Twenty-eight of the most influential Republican Senators favored some immediate change in the Cabinet. "You cannot change the President's character," said Fessenden, "or conduct, unfor-

---

[7] H. C. Bowen to Chase, September 13, 1862. Chase MSS.

[8] Fessenden, *Life and Letters of Fessenden*, p. 265.

[9] *Ibid.*, p. 264.

[10] Forbes to W. P. Fessenden, November 15, 1862; quoted in Hughes, *Forbes*, I, 338. It was known that Seward had not favored the Emancipation Proclamation. See Sedgwick to Forbes, December 22, 1862; quoted in Hughes, *op. cit.*, p. 344.

tunately; he remained long enough at Springfield surrounded by todies and office-seekers, to persuade himself
that he was especially chosen by the Almighty for this great
cause and well chosen."[11]

In April, 1864, even the *New York Times* burst forth in
violent criticism of the Government. "Gold at 175, and
Congress, with tax bills, tariff bills, bank bills, and every
financial measure lifeless and shapeless, engaged in putting
down debate in the National Capital. In the name of loyal
people we protest. It is a disgrace and an outrage. . . . By
their default the prices of everything that sustains life are
rapidly mounting. The currency is gradually turning into
worthless rags. Inch by inch, foot by foot, the government
moves on straight before the eyes of its guardians toward the
bottomless pit of bankruptcy."[12]   Richard Henry Dana
declared that the most striking thing about Washington politics in 1863 was the absence of loyalty to the President, and
he also believed the idea that Lincoln was incompetent was
so widespread that if the Republican national convention
were to be held then, he could not be renominated.[13]   To the
existing opposition, the suspension of the use of the writ of
habeas corpus, certain arbitrary arrests, and the suspension of
the press in various places added to the growing dissatisfaction.[14]   It was significant that when the Frémont party arose
it was based on those things as well as on the more direct
opposition to slavery.

In June of 1863, Montgomery Blair, in a speech at Concord, Massachusetts, attacked the radical elements in the
North, placing them on a level with the Confederates.[15]

---

[11] Nicolay and Hay, *Lincoln*, IV, 265 ff., gives an account of this affair. See also,
Pierce, *Life of Sumner*, IV. The best inside accounts are: Hughes, *Forbes*, I, 344,
and Fessenden, *Life of Fessenden*, pp. 231 ff.

[12] *New York Times*, April 13, 1864.

[13] Dana to Adams, March 9, 1863. Adams, *Dana*, II, 264.

[14] Esarey declares concerning Indiana that "politics" reached the low watermark
in 1863. The state government was almost in abeyance. "Federal provost marshals,
marshals, recruiting officers, detectives, draft officers, and quartermasters . . . disre-
garded the ordinary police and judicial system of the state." *History of Indiana*,
II, 798. See also the *Crisis* (Columbus, Ohio), June 10, 17, and July 3, 1863.

[15] *Liberator*, June 26, 1863.

This was a signal for renewed hostility to the Blair faction, which was thought to be the leading spirit of the conservative forces at Washington.[16] Thaddeus Stevens declared that if the President was going to retain Blair in his Cabinet it was time for the people to look for a successor.[17] Although he did not designate anyone, presumably he had either Chase or Frémont in mind. It was said, although probably with some exaggeration, that at the end of the Thirty-seventh Congress, only two of its members supported Lincoln.[18] Early in 1864, Senator Trumbull declared that although the desire for the President's re-election seemed to be quite general, in reality it was only on the surface, for surprisingly few men at Washington desired it. There was a fear, he said, that the President was too undecided and inefficient to put down the rebellion.[19] Trumbull correctly represented the radical Republican sentiment of Illinois, for it was feared that some of the leading journals might join the opposition.[20] It is important to note that this opposition to the administration which is being considered is quite apart from the regular Democratic forces and is within the center of the Republican party itself.

The opposition to the President gradually centered about Secretary Chase and General Frémont, and grew into presidential booms for each of them. It is important to note, therefore, the movement for Chase; for, if he had become the established candidate of the radicals, Frémont's following would have been unimportant. As early as January, 1862, a direct effort was started to organize support for a Chase movement for the presidency in 1864.[21] In May of that year Chase began to criticize the President's modification of General Hunter's proclamation[22] and his retention of

---

[16] *New York Tribune,* October 14, 1863; *Anti-Slavery Standard,* July 4, 1863.
[17] Stevens to Chase, October 8, 1863, Chase MSS (Pa. Hist. Soc.). See also McClure, *Pennsylvania,* p. 255.
[18] Riddle, *Life of Wade,* p. 255.
[19] Trumbull to Pike, February 6, 1864. Trumbull MSS.
[20] Cole, *Era of the Civil War,* p. 315.
[21] James Stone to Chase, January 15, 1862. Chase MSS.
[22] Hunter's proclamation freed the slaves in his military area.

McClellan as Commander of the Army of Virginia.[23]   He found fault with the way in which the Government was administered,[24] and began to court the friendship of the *New York Tribune*.[25]   It was common knowledge that many people looked upon Chase as the only Cabinet member who favored a vigorous prosecution of the war,[26] and by the end of 1862 it was well known that he might be a candidate in 1864.[27]   Horace Greeley declared that Chase would be his first choice,[28] and Chase let it be known that he would accept the honor if it came his way.[29]

The important point to keep in mind, however, is that by the end of 1863, there was a considerable group of Republicans who opposed Lincoln's re-election and were ready to support Chase or someone else if Chase did not seem to be the best choice.[30]   An illustration of how ardently Chase worked for the presidential nomination is seen in his relations with Jay Cooke.[31]   Chase suggested that financial articles could be printed in the journals of the country, and with them the casual statement that the success of the Government in financial matters was due to the fact that Chase had secured the adoption of sound measures.[32]   Jay Cooke endeavored to follow this suggestion and to secure the aid of other bankers.[33]   As a result there appeared from time to

---

[23] Chase to Greeley, May 21, 1862. Chase MSS (N. Y. Pub. Lib.).

[24] Chase to [   ], September 7, 1862. Chase MSS (N. Y. Pub. Lib.).

[25] Chase to Greeley, May 21, 1862. Chase MSS (N. Y. Pub. Lib.).

[26] See Garfield Letters, September 20, 1862; quoted in Smith, *Garfield*, I, 238.

[27] Jay Cooke to Chase, September 25, 1862.   Chase MSS (N. Y. Pub. Lib.) explains how the story was being circulated.

[28] Greeley to Chase, September 29, 1863. Chase MSS (Pa. Hist. Soc.).

[29] Chase to Greeley, October 9, 1863. Chase MSS (Pa. Hist. Soc.).

[30] Thomas Heaton to Chase, October 19, 1863. Chase MSS (Pa. Hist. Soc.). See also Barber to Trumbull, October 30, 1863, Trumbull MSS. Barber said, "I have been for some time aware that measures upon an extensive scale are being adopted to nominate some other man for President. The causes for this movement are patent to you as to any other of our leading statesmen." Brown to Trumbull, November 12, 1863, Trumbull MSS. Brown thought that Blair was retained by Lincoln as an antidote to Chase.

[31] Cooke was a New York banker who aided Chase in financial affairs.

[32] Henry Cooke to Jay Cooke, March 25, 1863; quoted in Oberholtzer, *Jay Cooke*, I, 360.

[33] Joshua Hanna to Cooke, December 1, 1863; quoted in Oberholtzer, *op. cit.*, p. 363.

time short articles which congratulated Chase on his banking policies.[34]

Simultaneously with the growth of the opposition to the President as centered about Chase, there developed a less completely organized effort to present the name of Frémont. There had been a more or less widespread belief that he had been unfairly dealt with by the administration.[35]

In May, 1863, it became known—to a small group of people at least—that Frémont was going to present himself as a presidential candidate.[36] The friends of Chase believed that whatever enthusiasm there was for Frémont indicated hostility toward Lincoln, and that in the long run it would aid the cause of Chase.[37] The fact that there were constant rumors that Frémont would be returned to active duty may have retarded his presidential boom. As his support developed later, it came from the German population and the abolitionists. A meeting of the former was held at Cleveland, October 20, 1863, and a platform was presented which foreshadowed that of the Cleveland convention which nominated Frémont in 1864.[38] The abolitionist support of Frémont was noted in the speeches which Wendell Phillips delivered at various times in 1863, and in which he denounced both Lincoln and Chase and praised Frémont.[39]

Thus, by 1864, the rift in the Republican party which had shown itself in 1861, had been considerably widened. As the *Boston Transcript* stated: "Individualism, a furious hatred of some particular man and an equally furious liking for others, is beginning to show itself among the Republicans in a manner destructive to common sense, and destructive to

---

[34] An example is as follows: "Secretary Chase has shown his great wisdom and forecast in bringing forth his scheme, and he has saved the country, and made a name for himself that will live forever." *Iowa City Republican*, December 23, 1863. See also Leavitt to Chase, September 30, 1863; Moore to Chase, September 23, 1863; Chester to Chase, June 22, 1863; Heaton to Chase, September 2, 1863. Chase MSS.

[35] *New York Semi-Weekly Tribune*, March 25, 1863.

[36] Brown to Chase, May 25, 1863. Chase MSS.

[37] B. R. Plumley to Chase, October 3, 1863. Chase MSS.

[38] *Cleveland Herald*, October 21, 1863; the *Crisis*, October 20, 1863. The Germans of St. Louis never ceased to be ardent Frémont men. See Woodruff to Chase, October 4, 1863. Chase MSS.

[39] *Liberator*, July 4, November 20, 1863; *New York Times*, December 23, 1863.

the principle of political combination."[40] The *National Anti-Slavery Standard* announced that its position would be one of "masterly inactivity as between the factions that supported Lincoln, Frémont, or Chase."[41]

The movements for Chase and Frémont were developing simultaneously. The friends of Chase continued to urge him for the presidency, and among his most active advocates was Jay Cooke. He could well afford to support Chase because he had made a clear profit of $200,000 out of his handling of the five-twenty loan.[42] He and his brother sought campaign funds, secured the publication of articles in support of Chase, and gave financial backing for the establishment of a Chase newspaper.[43] It was said that Chase was more popular in Washington than Lincoln, and that the success which he had had in securing funds for the war was the only success that the administration had experienced.[44]

The Chase movement in Washington was sponsored by a group of men, both Congressmen and private citizens, who, on February 20, 1864, published a manifesto known as the Pomeroy Circular.[45] This manifesto stated that the interests of the country and of freedom demanded a change in the administration in favor of "vigor, purity, and nationality"; that if President Lincoln were nominated for a second term he could not be elected; and that Chase possessed the qualities requisite for the needs of the country during the next four years. The *New York Tribune* took note of the manifesto, printed an extensive history of the achievements of Chase as Secretary of the Treasury, and declared that he deserved the generous consideration of the people.[46]

Although there were some favorable reactions to the movement for Chase, he was paying close attention to the

---

[40] February 27, 1864.   [41] April 2, 1864.   [42] Oberholtzer, *Jay Cooke*, I, 325.
[43] *Ibid.*, pp. 364-65. Henry Cooke spent $10,000 in the Chase cause and Jay Cooke spent as much as $2,000 for one article favoring Chase which appeared in the *Atlantic Monthly*.
[44] Doster, *Lincoln and the Civil War*, p. 173.
[45] Printed in *New York Times*, February 23, 1864; *New York Tribune*, February 24, 1864.
[46] *New York Tribune*, February 24, 1864.

developments in Ohio, which he thought would be a good indication of popular feeling.[47]   He already knew that the *Cincinnati Gazette* was unfavorable to him and that the *Cincinnati Commercial* was less friendly than it had been.[48] The lower house of the Ohio General Assembly had already passed a resolution declaring adherence to the emancipation and amnesty proclamations of the President,[49] and there was a rumor that a resolution would be introduced favoring his re-election.[50] The introduction of such a resolution would be almost tantamount to its passage, because the Republicans could scarcely admit what the Democrats had been contending, that Lincoln was a failure.[51] The friends of Chase were able, for a time, to prevent the introduction of a resolution of that sort either in the Legislature or in the Republican state caucus;[52] but the Pomeroy Circular brought the matter to a head in Ohio.[53]

A caucus which was held on February 25 passed a resolution favoring the re-election of Lincoln,[54] and the Chase men either rallied to its support or remained away from the caucus.[55] A similar situation existed in Indiana, where it was claimed that in the General Assembly the Republican members from five of the eleven congressional districts opposed the introduction of a resolution favoring Lincoln's re-election.[56] Such a resolution was introduced, however, and passed February 23,[57] and thus the Republicans of Ohio and Indiana declared for Lincoln.

---

[47] T. Alger to Chase, February 25, 1864. Chase MSS.

[48] T. Heaton to Chase, January 14, 1864. Chase MSS (Pa. Hist. Soc.).

[49] *Journal of the House of Representatives, State of Ohio,* Fifty-sixth General Assembly, LX, 118.

[50] A. P. Stone to Chase, February 4, 1864. Chase MSS.   [51] *Ibid.*

[52] W. D. Lindsley to Chase, February 9, 1864; L. R. Grunckel to Chase, February 12, 1864. Chase MSS. These letters explain the situation in Ohio.

[53] Parsons to Chase, March 2, 1864. Chase MSS.

[54] *Cleveland Leader,* February 29, 1864.

[55] *Cincinnati Enquirer,* February 20, 1864. Parsons thought that all the Chase men remained away. See Parsons to Chase, March 2, 1864, Chase MSS; the *New York Tribune* (February 26) said that forty-two out of a hundred and five Republicans remained away and the *Cleveland Leader* (February 29) said seventeen out of a hundred and seven remained away.

[56] *Intelligencer,* February 27, 1864.

[57] *Ibid.,* February 25, 1864.

Chase was in a quandary. He was inclined to think that the nomination of Lincoln was certain. But he was so thoroughly out of sympathy with the President's stand in regard to nearly all public policies and he so detested Blair and Weed, who seemed to him to control Lincoln, that he was loath to give up the race.[58] He submitted the question to Horace Greeley,[59] who replied that, although a day previously he had believed that Chase should make an open announcement of his candidacy, he now thought that Chase should make an announcement that he was not a candidate.[60] At the same time Chase learned that his friends in Cleveland, Ohio, did not think that he could successfully combat Lincoln,[61] that his friends in Cincinnati were in a quandary to know what to do,[62] and that many politicians thought he should withdraw his name because division in the party was doing harm to its chances for success.[63] Chase, therefore, formally withdrew from the presidential race.[64] The *New York Tribune* did not entirely give up the idea of the Chase candidacy,[65] and there was a slight continuance of the movement for him,[66] but it had reached its zenith in February and was not seriously revived after Chase's own agreement that it was unwise.[67]

The formal withdrawal of Chase did not unite the party. There were Republicans of prominence like C. F. Adams and Thaddeus Stevens who did not like Chase any better than Lincoln and were completely out of sympathy with his

[58] These views were clearly set down in a letter to James A. Hamilton, February 29, 1864. Chase MSS (N. Y. Pub. Lib.).

[59] Chase to Greeley, February 29, 1864. Chase MSS (N. Y. Pub. Lib.).

[60] Greeley to Chase, March 2, 1864. Chase MSS (Pa. Hist. Soc. Lib.). Chase also asked the opinion of Henry Cooke. See Oberholtzer, *Jay Cooke*, I, 362.

[61] Parsons to Chase, March 2, 1864. Chase MSS.

[62] Mellen to Chase, March 2, 1864. Chase MSS.

[63] Garfield was among those. Smith, *Garfield*, I, 375.

[64] Chase to James Hall, March 5, 1864, quoted in *New York Tribune*, March 11, 1864, *Boston Transcript*, same date, and elsewhere.

[65] *New York Tribune*, March 11, 1864.

[66] There was talk of a Chase convention to be held at Philadelphia, similar to the Cleveland Frémont convention. See *Cleveland Leader*, May 27, 1864.

[67] There was a movement to swing the Republican convention for him, but it was not widespread. See Ayer to Judge Stickney, May 25, 1864. Chase MSS (Pa. Hist. Soc.).

financial program.[68]   James A. Garfield, who had urged
Chase to withdraw for the sake of party harmony, had
decided a month later that Lincoln could not possibly be
re-elected and declared that he did not know a dozen men
who thought otherwise.[69]   It is evident that the opposition
to Lincoln within his party was widespread and that it was
apparently on the increase.   The more radical Republicans
of Wisconsin believed that the President was too much
influenced by such men as Blair and Bates,[70] and a similar
belief was current in Connecticut.[71]   It was declared that the
majority of the members of the Legislature of New York
opposed his re-election, and that the New York Congressmen held the same opinion.[72]   Then there was the Chase
following some of whom, at least, were willing to support
anyone who seemed likely to oppose Lincoln successfully.[73]
The Lincoln press took note of the rising anti-Lincoln sentiment and warned the party that it was merely the work of
disappointed office-seekers.[74]

In this situation Frémont or any other ambitious political
aspirant might well have scanned the political horizon of
1864, with the conclusion that the times were propitious for
the success of a popular candidate.   General B. F. Butler,
who had political aspirations, was informed that, notwithstanding the course taken by Chase, there was a "strong sentiment in favor of a more efficient man" than President Lincoln.[75]   In Connecticut, although Secretary Welles had
attempted to deter the party leaders from thinking of a "new
candidate,"[76] the idea persisted that the President was fol-

---

[68] C. F. Adams to Forbes, March 3, 1864; quoted in Hughes, *Forbes*, II, 85; the
Crisis, March 23, 1864.
[69] Garfield to Rhodes, April 28, 1864; quoted in Smith, *Garfield*, I, 376.
[70] John F. Potter to Elihu Washburn, April 16 and May 14, 1864.   E. Washburn MSS.   [71] C. Day to Welles, January 22, 1864.   Welles MSS.
[72] Editorial, *New York Evening Post*, March 8, 1864.   The *Post* declared that
the Lincoln clubs which were being organized were made up of office-holders and did
not represent public opinion.
[73] Governor Yates of Illinois was one.   See W. P. Mellen to Chase, March,
1864.   Chase MSS (Pa. Hist. Soc.).
[74] See *Cleveland Leader*, March 4, 1864.
[75] Wentworth to Butler, March 13, 1864.   *B. F. Butler Correspondence*, III, 513.
[76] Gideon Welles to E. T. Welles, January 12, 1864.   Welles MSS.

lowing a "drifting, conciliatory, and temporizing" policy, which, if it did not ruin the country before the war ended, would do so afterward when the guidance of an earnest anti-slavery man was needed.[77] The *New York Times,* always an administration paper, noticed that the opposition to Lincoln was strong enough to encourage the running of a candidate, even though Lincoln were nominated by the regular convention.[78]

---

[77] Howard to Welles, May 30, 1864. Welles MSS. Howard thought that Lincoln would be nominated but that unless he changed his cabinet and adopted a more radical policy he could not be elected.

[78] March 5, 1864.

CHAPTER VIII

THE NOMINATION OF FRÉMONT
1864

The movement in support of Frémont as a successor to Lincoln probably started in Missouri, which had been a hotbed of Republican radicalism ever since the removal of Frémont from command in the west in 1861. W. C. Bryant in a New York speech declared that the true party of Missouri was the radical party, that its principles were identical with those laid down by Frémont in 1861, and that their cause was that of the whole nation.[1] The influence of the radicals in Missouri was shown by the fact that the State Legislature voted adversely on a resolution favoring the re-election of President Lincoln, and in a similar manner on one indorsing his administration.[2]

In 1863, B. Gratz Brown, several radical Congressmen, and two members of the Missouri Legislature, sponsored a meeting to be held at Louisville, Kentucky, to discuss a method for the extermination of slavery. The meeting, which was to have been held January 8, was postponed until February 22, 1864.[3] In the meantime, the *Boston Pioneer*, which had been declared the official organ of the German convention at Cleveland in 1863, began to support Frémont as the only true candidate for the presidency.[4]

The Louisville convention assembled with about one hundred and twenty-five delegates from four states: Mis-

---

[1] Bryant at Cooper Institute, October 2, 1863; quoted in the *Crisis*, October 14, 1863.

[2] On the first resolution thirty-seven favored his re-election and forty-five opposed. On the second, thirty-three wished to indorse the administration and forty-six opposed. The vote was taken February 19, 1864. See *New York Tribune*, February 24, 1864.

[3] *New York Tribune*, January 22, 1864.

[4] Quoted in *Cincinnati Enquirer*, February 12, 1864. Caspar Butz declared that the Germans controlled 400,000 votes. See speech of Butz, quoted in *Cincinnati Enquirer*, February 23, 1864.

souri, Arkansas, Tennessee, and Kentucky.[5]   The delegates
were clearly divided into two groups—those who would not
support Lincoln at all, and those who simply desired to force
him to adopt a more radical policy in regard to slavery.
Resolutions were adopted declaring opposition to the existence of slavery, opposing the Amnesty Proclamation, and
favoring the one-term principle.[6]   The division of the convention was demonstrated when a resolution was presented
calling a new convention to meet at St. Louis on May 10.
The Kentucky element declared that they understood that
the Louisville convention was merely to start antislavery
agitation, while the Missouri delegates wanted to nominate
Frémont.   They were willing to abide the decision of the
regular Republican convention as far as a candidate was concerned, and would take no part in any other movement.[7]
The vote on the matter of the St. Louis convention was a
victory for the Kentucky element, and therefore nothing was
accomplished at Louisville by Fremont's friends.[8]

The Missouri delegates returned to St. Louis, and on
March 2 they decided to support Frémont, to hold a meeting
on May 10, and to appoint a committee to arrange for a
national convention.[9]   The following day the *Westliche Post*
and the *Neue Zeit* announced that they would support Frémont.[10]   The *Westliche Post* declared that there had been
enough secret agitation and that the time had come when
the radical party of the United States should act openly.

In Illinois the Frémont workers were not less active than
in Missouri.   The *Chicago Tribune* noticed that Frémont
was to be a candidate whether nominated by the regular
Republican convention or not.[11]   The *New York Tribune*, in

---

[5] *Cincinnati Enquirer*, February 23, 1864; *New York Tribune*, March 5, 1864.
[6] *New York Tribune*, March 5, 1864.
[7] *Ibid.*; also, *Cincinnati Enquirer*, February 24, 1864.
[8] *Ibid.*   Fifty-three delegates favored the St. Louis convention and sixty-four opposed it.
[9] *Cincinnati Enquirer*, March 8, 1864.
[10] Quoted in *Cincinnati Enquirer*, March 7, 1864. The *New York Tribune* noted the fact March 4. The *Westliche Post* had opposed Lincoln for a long time. See Laughlin, *Missouri Politics*, p. 145.
[11] *Chicago Tribune*, quoted in *Cleveland Leader*, February 15, 1864.

mentioning the widespread opposition to the re-election of Lincoln, pointed to the liberal German element in Illinois and mentioned a Chicago journal edited by Caspar Butz.[12] That journal was the *Deutsche Amerikanische Monatsschrift* which was modeled after the fashion of the *Atlantic Monthly*, and counted among its contributors such men as Schurz and Siegel.[13]   The conservative *New York Times* printed letters from Chicago which set forth the growing disaffection for the President.[14]   The *Chicago Telegraph* came out for Frémont, declaring that he was the true lover of liberty;[15] and although the *Chicago Journal* and the *Chicago Tribune* announced their support for Lincoln, they did so with some apology and explanation.[16]   In March the German Workingmen's Association held a meeting at which Emil Pretorius, Moss of Missouri, and Caspar Butz urged the qualities which made Frémont the true leader of the people.[17]   Resolutions were passed declaring that the great patronage power of the President made it unsafe for the people to allow him to hold office during a second term and that Frémont was the choice of the German citizens.   During the month of April the Chicago Frémont Club was organized under the leadership of Caspar Butz, and a call was sent to all the "Radical Germans of the State of Illinois" to meet at Springfield on May 24.[18]

In May, the Springfield *Staats Anzeiger* came out in opposition to the President, declaring that it would protest his election at all costs.[19]   Frémont clubs were formed by the Germans at various places in Illinois, and the similarity of the resolutions which were adopted shows that some state-wide organizing influence was at work.   In general they advocated that slavery should be abolished, that the Confed-

---

[12] February 27, 1864.
[13] *Ibid.*; also Cole, *Era of the Civil War*, p. 317.
[14] March 13, 1864.
[15] March 30, quoted in *Cincinnati Enquirer*, April 6, 1864.
[16] *Chicago Journal* quoted in *New Nation*, May 14, 1864; and *Tribune*, quoted in *Liberator*, March 18, 1864.
[17] *Cincinnati Enquirer*, March 31, 1864.
[18] *Ibid.*, April 20, 1864; *New Nation*, April 9, 1864.
[19] *Ibid.*, May 14, 1864.

erate states should be treated as territories, that a national school system should be established, and that the one-term principle should be adopted.[20]   The *Mississippi Blätter* and the *Highland Union* (German) came out for Frémont; and, in fact, the *Illinois Staats Zeitung* was probably the only German paper in Illinois for Lincoln.[21] The show of strength came at the meeting of the state Republican convention. Although resolutions were adopted indorsing Lincoln for a second term, the convention was almost evenly divided on that point, and the Frémont men were determined to support their candidate independently.

In Iowa the *Staats Zeitung,* published at Dubuque, was the leader of the Frémont Germans.   It declared that the Chase and Butler men, as well as the war Democrats and radicals, would support him.[22]   In Wisconsin Emil Pretorius organized Frémont clubs;[23] and, according to the *Cleveland Herald,* all of the German papers of that state favored Frémont.[24]   It was declared that the Frémont support in Wisconsin, while not strong enough to elect Frémont, was potent enough to defeat Lincoln.[25]   In Indiana clubs were organized which at first supported Chase and Frémont;[26] later the *Free Press* and the *Helvetia* raised the Frémont banner.[27] Although it was declared that in the Republican state convention of Indiana the resolution indorsing Lincoln was adopted without calling for the negative vote,[28] there was a contest similar to that in Illinois, but apparently with less Frémont strength.

New York City was the center of an active group of Frémont workers. The movement for him appeared openly in February, 1864;[29] and in March a Frémont journal, the

---

[20] See *New Nation,* May 21, 1864, for resolutions passed at Peoria and at Alton.

[21] Cole, *Era of Civil War,* p. 316; also, *New Nation,* May 21, 1864.

[22] *Staats Zeitung;* quoted in *Cincinnati Enquirer,* March 26, 1864.   Its editor was Gustavus Grahl. See Grahl to Chase, March 7, 1864.   Chase MSS.

[23] *New Nation,* May 21, 1864.   [24] Quoted, *Ibid.,* May 14, 1864.

[25] Booth to Chase, May 2, 1864.   Chase MSS.

[26] Rudsill to Chase, February 4, 1864.   Chase MSS.

[27] *New Nation,* April 2, May 14, 1864.

[28] *Cincinnati Enquirer,* February 25, 1864.

[29] *New York Tribune,* February 23, 24, 29, 1864.

New Nation, was established.[30] This journal was edited by
a former staff officer of Frémont's, and announced that it
would endeavor to secure liberty for all, the maintenance of
the Monroe Doctrine, a more efficient military organization,
national education, and reorganization of the government
whereby the executive department would be more responsible to the legislative power.[31] It advocated a greater nationality, a "New Nation," which could be achieved only by the
complete overthrow of slavery.   Besides the *New Nation*, a
German paper printed in English, the *German American*,
began to support Frémont,[32] and the *New York Independent* declared that Frémont men were working night and
day in his behalf.[33]

A New York Frémont Club was formally organized
March 18.   The chairman declared that if Frémont were
elected he would put down the rebellion, make Confederate
property pay for the war, abolish slavery, and issue an
amnesty proclamation less lenient to the Confederates than
the one which existed.[34]   Horace Greeley addressed the
meeting.   He declared that while he would support the
regular party nomination, Frémont would be acceptable.
The *Albany Standard and Statesman* reported a remarkable
movement for the organization of Frémont clubs, and while
it thought the Frémont movement was premature, it declared
that it was forced to be so on account of the action of the
administration in attempting through office-holders to secure
the support of state conventions and legislatures.[35]   Frémont
was in New York at the time, and although he was busily
engaged in furthering his interests, few of his letters are
preserved.   According to his belief, this is partly due to the

---

[30] The initial number appeared March 5, 1864.
[31] The editor was General Cluseret. See *New Nation*, March 5, 19, 1864.
[32] *Cincinnati Enquirer*, March 18, 1864.
[33] Quoted in the *Intelligencer*, March 19, 1864.
[34] *New York Tribune*, March 19, 1864.
[35] Quoted in *New York Tribune*, April 1, 1864. The *New Nation* declared that
great progress was being made in the organization of Frémont clubs. See edition of
May 7, 1864.   Thurlow Weed later declared that Horace Greeley wrote letters to
people all over New England in furtherance of the Frémont movement. See Weed,
What I Know About Greeley, p. 13.

fact that the post-office officials tampered with his mail so that much of it never reached its destination.[36]

In New Jersey the German National Clubs held a convention at Newark, February 10, and agreed to support either Frémont or Butler.[37]   A Frémont meeting was held in Pittsburgh in April, and while the names of its leaders indicate that it was predominantly German in character, there were various other elements present.[38]

In New England there were two important Frémont groups. The German group was ably led by Heinzen of the *Boston Pioneer*,[39] and Wendell Phillips was the outstanding Frémont leader among the abolitionists.[40]   The latter, in a Cooper Institute address in December, 1863, declared that peace could not be restored until Butler or Frémont "manned the guns."   At the annual meeting of the Massachusetts Anti-Slavery Society, Phillips introduced a resolution in opposition to Lincoln.[41]   Garrison opposed the Frémont movement because the latter had shown no interest in Lincoln's Emancipation Proclamation; but the Phillips resolution was adopted by the society.[42]

It seems, therefore, that the support for Frémont was making some headway during March and April of 1864. The Chase men were reluctant to return to the Lincoln camp.[43]   Many of the Germans were ardent Frémont men,[44] and probably half of the abolitionists were following his standard.[45]   Although, on the eve of the convention which

---

[36] Frémont to Simon Stevens, March 15, 1864.   Frémont MSS (New York Pub. Lib.).

[37] *New York Tribune*, February 27, 1864.

[38] *New Nation*, April 16, 1864.   See also Schamberg to Chase, March 16, 1864.

[39] *Cincinnati Enquirer*, March 5, 1864.   [40] *Liberator*, January 1, 1864.

[41] *Liberator*, February 5, 1864.   The meeting was held January 28, 1864.   No record of the votes was taken.   Phillips made frequent speeches against Lincoln.   See *Liberator*, May 20, 1864; the *New Nation*, May 28, 1864.

[42] *Liberator*, February 5, 1864.

[43] Heaton to Chase, April 2, 1864.   Chase MSS.

[44] Some German papers remained Democratic, but Welles declared that the Germans were "transcendentally" for Frémont.   See Welles to [   ], February 28, 1864, Welles MSS.   See the list of German Frémont journals in *New Nation*, April 4, 1864.

[45] This estimate is based on the vote for the Phillips resolution adopted by the Massachusetts Anti-Slavery Society.

nominated Frémont for the presidency, his followers represented but a fragment of the Republican party, there seemed
to be a growing feeling that his candidacy together with the
general lack of enthusiasm for Lincoln would cause the
defeat of the latter.[46]

The Missouri delegates to the Louisville convention of
February, 1864, began to arrange for a new radical Republican convention which would consider the question of select-
ing a candidate for the presidency,[47] and it was announced
that such a meeting would be held at Cleveland on May 10.[48]
Plans were changed, however, and various calls appeared for
a meeting to be held at Cleveland, May 31.

The first call, that of the "People's Provisional Committee," was sent out by the Frémont Club of New York,
and was dated May 6. It declared that it was time for all
independent men to confer together to resist the unrestricted
use of the patronage which was about to destroy the rights
of the people.[49] A second call was signed by some of the
officials of the state of New York.[50] It summoned those who
believed that the rebellion could be suppressed without the
necessity of infringing upon the rights of individuals, and
that the extinction of slavery was one of the practical effects
of the war.[51] The third call was signed by a good many
abolitionists. Its distinctive feature was the demand for
"such a plan of reconstruction as should conform entirely to
the policy of freedom for all, placing political power alone
in the hands of the loyal, executing with vigor the law for
the confiscation of property of rebels."[52] The *New Nation*
urged the workingmen to send delegates to Cleveland, declaring that speculators and contractors had ground down

[46] Baldwin to Trumbull, April 4, 1864, Trumbull MSS; Forbes to Curtis, April
28, 1864, quoted in Hughes, *Curtis*, II, 86. The situation was well summarized in
the *New York Evening Post*, May 25, 1864.
[47] See above, p. 96.
[48] *Cleveland Leader*, March 7, 1864.
[49] *New York Tribune*, May 24, 1864.
[50] Lucius Robinson and John Cochran were prominent.
[51] Appeared about May 18. See *Boston Transcript, Intelligencer, Crisis*, for
that date.
[52] *New York Tribune*, May 24, 1864.

the people, but that now they could show their power.[53]
Thus an attempt was made to secure the support of the Germans, abolitionists, and radical Republicans, and in the case
of the second call, the war Democrats.

The Republican journals, as a general thing, published
one or all of the calls; and the Democratic press pointed to
the Cleveland convention as an indication of dissension
within the Republican ranks.[54] The *New York Herald*,
which opposed nominating conventions, declared that a mass
meeting such as the Cleveland convention would be, was a
good thing and should be well attended.[55] The *New York
Tribune* pretended to regard it as an advisory body only, and
as such, those who favored it would not be bound by its
decisions.[56] It was known, however, that in all probability
the Cleveland meeting would nominate Frémont for the
presidency,[57] and the Lincoln press was inclined to condemn
it.[58] Some of the Chase men endeavored to have it postponed until the day before the regular Republican convention, and then have it meet at Baltimore, where it would be
useful as an influence over the action of the Republican
convention.[59]

The convention which met at Cleveland on May 31, was
a mass meeting, not unlike the Republican meeting at Pittsburgh in 1856. Frémont supporters met at various places
and sent delegates but with no common scheme of represen-
tation.[60] About four hundred delegates were present, mostly
from Illinois, Iowa, Ohio, Pennsylvania, and Missouri,
although nearly every Northern state was represented.[61]
It is clear that the leaders did not want it to appear as a

---

[53] May 7, 1864.

[54] *Boston Transcript*, May 30; *Detroit Tribune*, May 25; *Cleveland Leader*, May
19; *Crisis*, May 18, 1864.

[55] Quoted in *New Nation*, May 21, 1864.

[56] May 28, 1864.

[57] *New York Evening Post*, May 25, 1864.

[58] See *Cleveland Leader*, May 19, 1864.

[59] Mullett to Chase, May 16, 1864, Chase MSS; also *Cleveland Leader*, May 27,
1864; *New Nation*, May 21, 1864.

[60] *Boston Transcript*, May 30; *New York Tribune*, May 31; *Cleveland Leader*,
May 25; *New Nation*, May 21, 1864.

[61] *New York Tribune*, May 31; *Crisis*, June 8, 1864.

German gathering, and, although B. Gratz Brown of Illinois was the most active leader, the president of the New York Frémont Club called the meeting to order, ex-Governor Johnson of Pennsylvania was the temporary chairman, and John Cochrane was the president.[62]   In the opening address Cochrane declared that the administration was not capable of bringing the war to a successful termination, and that the freedom of speech and of the press was being endangered.[63]

It soon appeared that there were two factions at Cleveland—a small group, mostly from the East, who favored the nomination of General Grant, and a larger group who supported Frémont.[64]   The Grant faction attempted to get the convention to postpone the nomination of a candidate, but a motion to that effect was defeated,[65] and a motion that the convention should vote by states met with a similar fate. The majority of the delegates had assembled for one definite purpose, the nomination of Frémont, and that they accomplished with great enthusiasm.   John Cochrane was chosen as the vice-presidential candidate.[66]

The platform resolutions declared that the right of free speech, free press, and *habeas corpus* should be maintained save in districts where martial law had been proclaimed; that slavery should be destroyed by a constitutional amendment; that the Monroe Doctrine should be defended; that the president and vice-president should be elected by direct vote of the people, and for one term only; that reconstruction was the function of Congress and not of the president; and "that the confiscation of the lands of the rebels and their distribution among soldiers and actual settlers" would be a measure of justice.[67]

---

[62] *Crisis*, May 18; *Cleveland Leader*, June 1, 1864.

[63] Cochrane believed in 1860 that the North was responsible for the conditions that drove the South to secession.   Then after the opening of the War he supported the North, but became a critic of the President.   See Alexander, *Political History of New York*, III, 4, 6, 9; also *New York Tribune*, March 16, 1861.

[64] *Cleveland Leader*, June 1, 1864.

[65] It received but nine favorable votes.

[66] *Cleveland Leader*, June 1, 1864.

[67] *Cleveland Leader*, June 2, 1864.   A convenient place to find the platform is in the *American Annual Cyclopedia* for 1864, p. 786.

Frémont accepted the nomination with some qualification. He declared that the Cleveland convention was a protest against the acts of the administration in usurping extravagant powers and violating the constitutional rights of the people. It was, he said, a declaration of the right of the people to have candidates of their own choice. He did not agree, however, with the idea of a general confiscation of property as a measure of reconstruction, because he thought the idea of vengeance should not predominate. Furthermore, he declared that if the Republicans would nominate a candidate whose past actions showed fidelity to the principles announced at Cleveland, there would be no need for further protest, but that if Lincoln were nominated, then the protest would have to be continued.[68]

The Cleveland convention and the Frémont acceptance drew various comments from the press. The *Cleveland Herald* declared that the convention was made up of "sly politicians from New York, impetuous hair-brained Germans from St. Louis, abolitionists, and personal friends and parasites of Frémont."[69] The *Boston Transcript* spoke of it as an "informal gathering of Germans, radicals, and war Democrats,"[70] while the *Cincinnati Commercial* said that the "long-haired radicals" had called a meeting at Cleveland because they could not afford to go to Baltimore.[71] The *New York Times* considered the meeting as "diverting by-play" attended by an occasional philosopher who would study the movement as a form of mental hallucination.[72] The *Columbus Express* admitted that the platform was good but denounced the people who drew it up.[73] As a general thing, the Democratic journals printed the account of the convention, and pointed to it as an example of the fact that their declarations concerning freedom of speech and the like were being recognized—even adopted by other parties.[74]

---

[68] *New York Tribune,* June 6; *Ohio State Journal,* June 7, 1864.
[69] June 2, 1864.
[70] May 31, June 1, 1864.   [72] June 2, 1864.
[71] May 25, 1864.   [73] June 1, 1864.
[74] See the *Crisis,* and quotings of June 3, 1864; *Cleveland Leader,* June 3, 1864.

It was notable that in his letter of acceptance Frémont did not take a radical stand. The only radical part of the Cleveland platform was that concerning the confiscation of Confederate property, and that part Frémont renounced. Since he made a direct attack on the President, the *Boston Transcript* could see in the Frémont movement only the working out of a personal grudge.[75] His letter of acceptance also lent itself easily to the charge that he was seeking an alliance with the Democrats. Various journals pointed to that fact,[76] and Gurwoski, who had considerable insight into the times, believed that Frémont was seeking the Democratic nomination.[77] Thurlow Weed characterized the movement as a "slimy intrigue,"[78] and some journals that had been favorable to Frémont began to support Lincoln more consistently when it became evident that there would be an independent movement.[79]

It is important to note that men like Senator Trumbull, Thaddeus Stevens, Secretary Chase, Horace Greeley, Senator Pomeroy, Governor Yates, and others who had political influence and who did not favor the re-election of Lincoln, took no open part at least in the Cleveland movement.[80] The Lincoln press immediately took up the slogan which was carried through the entire campaign, that of the need for party solidarity before anything else.[81]

During the early months of 1864 when the Chase and Frémont movements were in the making, there existed simultaneously a more carefully organized movement to gain support for Lincoln's re-election. Early in January his friends began to work to create the impression that public opinion demanded it.[82] A "Union Lincoln Association"

---

[75] June 6, 1864.

[76] *Ohio State Journal*, June 8; *National Anti-Slavery Standard*, June 18; *Boston Transcript*, June 1, 1864.   [77] Gurwoski, *Diary*, III, 251 (Note for June 8, 1864).

[78] Barnes, *Weed's Memoirs*, p. 446.

[79] *Iowa City Republican* is an example; see edition of June 8, 1864.

[80] See Harris, *Political Conflict*, p. 376.

[81] *New York Times*, June 2; *Ohio State Journal*, June 8; *Washington Republican*, June 3; *Boston Transcript*, June 6, 1864.

[82] Freese to Chase, January 23, 1864. Chase MSS. Freese was on the staff of the *State Gazette*, Trenton, New Jersey.

was formed in New York to work for his cause there,[83] and the *New York Times* and other journals began to say that "the public interest" required the continuance of the President in office, and that the popular mind was determined on his re-election.[84]

The tactics used by the Lincoln forces were to have state legislatures and conventions pass resolutions favoring his policies and thus create an opinion or demand for his re-election when the national convention met at Baltimore on June 7. Thus, during the month of January, the state Republican convention of New Hampshire, the California Legislature, the Republican caucus of the Pennsylvania Legislature, the Kansas Legislature, the Maryland House of Delegates, and the Wisconsin Lower House, all passed resolutions favoring the re-election of Lincoln. During February the Minnesota State Senate, the Connecticut Union Convention, the Rhode Island Lower House, the Indiana Legislature, and the Republican caucus of Ohio followed in like manner. The state conventions seemed to be generally controlled by office-holders and were adroitly managed in Lincoln's favor.[85] The "Union League" or "Loyal League," which claimed an astonishingly large membership, was an important item in the movement for Lincoln's re-election.[86] The Garrison following of the abolitionists supported Lincoln, mainly because of his Emancipation Proclamation,[87] and some of the Germans were led into his column when it appeared that Frémont would bolt the party.[88]

The early agitation for Lincoln had several direct results. In the first place it brought the Frémont movement to a head. At first many of those who supported Frémont did so

---

[83] *New York Times,* January 21, 1864. The *Times* was the only New York journal that consistently supported Lincoln in 1864, and its files contain all of the arguments in his favor.

[84] *New York Times,* January 15, 1864. See also quoting in *Cleveland Leader,* January 15, 1864.

[85] Bolles to Welles, February 18, 1864; also Day to Welles, February 18, 1864, Welles MSS, describes the way in which the Connecticut convention was handled.

[86] *Cleveland Leader,* March 2, 1864.   [87] *Liberator,* March 18, 1864.

[88] *New York Tribune,* March 19, 1864. See resolutions of a German meeting held at New York, March 18.

with the intention of making him the regular party nominee,[89] but when it became clear that he would stand but little
show at the Baltimore convention, the separate movement
was developed.[90]   In the second place it brought the Chase
movement out into the open.   The Pomeroy Circular declared that it was on account of the early Lincoln agitation
that those who did not favor him were forced to direct their
efforts openly toward the selection of some other man, rather
than to await the Baltimore convention.   The third result
was the attempt to have the Baltimore convention postponed.
The *New York Evening Post* was the leader in that movement.   It represented that Lincoln, Chase, Frémont, Grant,
and Butler were being considered in connection with the presidency, and that in the disorganized state of public opinion
it was not possible to make a choice which would represent
a united party.[91]   Other journals which were only lukewarm
in their support of Lincoln pointed out that it would be well
to await the results of the spring military movements, and
that it was better to pursue a cautious policy than to act
hastily and regret the action.[92]

Late in March a direct appeal was made to the Republican Executive Committee to postpone the convention until
September 1, 1864;[93] this appeal was supported by a good
many people and journals.[94]   The Lincoln press declared
that the movement for postponement was merely a scheme
to defeat Lincoln,[95] and that it was started at the instance of
those who favored Frémont.[96]   They argued that if the

[89] Note the Louisville meeting of February 22, 1864.
[90] *New Nation*, March 19; *Ohio State Journal*, April 20, 1864.   It is to be noted
that as late as March 5 the *New Nation* was not urging a separate Frémont movement.   See editions of March 12, 19, 26, April 16, May 21, 1864.
[91] February 23, 1864.   This journal continued to urge such a move.   See March
21, 1864.
[92] *Boston Transcript*, March 23; *Daily Intelligencer*, March 10, 1864.
[93] The appeal was signed by W. C. Bryant, George Opdyke, and others.   It is
conveniently found in the *American Annual Cyclopedia* for 1864, p. 785.
[94] Forbes to Curtis, quoted in Hughes, Forbes, II, 88; *New York Tribune*, April
1, 1864; *Troy Whig*, quoted in *Tribune*, April 1, 1864; *New York Independent*, quoted
in *New York Times*, April 8, 1864.
[95] *New York Times*, April 8, 1864; *Ohio State Journal*, April 20; *Cleveland
Leader*, April 8; *New York Tribune*, April 1, 1864.
[96] *New York Times*, April 21, 1864.

convention were postponed more internal dissensions would develop.[97]

In the meantime the work for Lincoln continued. The *New York Times* declared that the South claimed to have seceded on account of Lincoln's election, and that it was now looking anxiously for the North to defeat him and not only prove that he should not have been elected, but also put in power the Democrats, with whom peace negotiations could be started.[98] Lincoln's re-election, therefore, was coincident with the determination to suppress the rebellion. In May the Republican organizations of Vermont, New Jersey, and Massachusetts declared for Lincoln.[99]

When the Republican convention met at Baltimore on June 7, there was no open opposition to the nomination of Lincoln, with the exception of that of the Missouri delegation. Two sets of delegates were present from Missouri, one calling themselves the "Union Radicals" and the other the "Unconditional Union Delegates."[100] The former opposed the nomination of Lincoln and the latter favored it; but the committee on credentials recommended the admission of the "Union Radicals" and the convention adopted that recommendation by a vote of 440 to 4.[101] That was an adroit move on the part of the Lincoln forces, for, although these delegates voted for Grant, their vote did not affect the nomination of Lincoln, and, since they were not rejected by the Republicans, the Frémont movement did not gain the momentum in Missouri that it might otherwise have done.[102] After the convention Francis P. Blair, Jr., declared that the politicians did not desire the nomination of Lincoln, but they accepted it as a concession to the public sentiment of the nation.[103] H. D. White probably stated the situation correctly when he said that there was general feeling among the

---

[97] *Cleveland Leader*, April 28, 1864; *New York Times*, April 4, 1864.
[98] April 1, 1864. This was a common argument of the Republicans in 1864.
[99] *New York Evening Post*, May 18, 1864; *Tribune*, May 26; *New York Times*, May 21, 22, 28, 1864; Knapp, *New Jersey*, p. 138.
[100] *Daily Intelligencer*, June 8, 15, 1864.   [101] *Ibid.*, June 15, 1864.
[102] See Laughlin, *Missouri Politics*, p. 109.
[103] Blair to Captain Bart, June 30, 1864; quoted in *New Nation*, July 2, 1864.

Republicans that a failure to nominate Lincoln would have been a concession to the enemy.[104]

The important thing to note here in regard to the Republican convention is its declaration of principles.[105]   The Republican platform, to a considerable extent, followed that of the Cleveland convention.   The points concerning the Monroe Doctrine, the extinction of slavery, and the right of asylum were practically identical.   The Republicans, of course, could not condemn the abuse of the power to suspend the writ of *habeas corpus,* or the violation of the freedom of speech, for those points furnished the main materials for the Democratic opposition; but otherwise the platform was as radical as the Cleveland platform after Frémont had renounced the plank concerning reconstruction policy.   The Republicans again were very adroit in adopting a resolution which was so stated as to indicate that the President, if he were elected, would be expected to reorganize his Cabinet, in such a way as to make it less conservative.[106]

---

[104] White, *Autobiography,* p. 120.

[105] The platform is conveniently found in *American Annual Cyclopedia,* 1864, pp. 788-89.

[106] See *National Anti-Slavery Standard,* July 9, 1864.

CHAPTER IX

FACTIONAL STRUGGLES

Before the Baltimore convention it is probable that the Frémont movement had the good will, if not the open support, of many Republicans because they saw in it one weapon which might be used to defeat Lincoln. But after June 7 there seemed to be a tendency to close the party ranks. Thus, the *New York Tribune* declared that, although it did not want to disparage Frémont, there were only two issues before the people, and therefore there was no room for a third party.[1] Both parties agreed that the Union should be preserved; the question to be decided was whether it should be done with or without slavery.

Administration journalists and other writers who had opposed Lincoln began to declare that Frémont was in league with the Democrats and wanted to secure the nomination by the Democratic party. The *Anti-Slavery Standard* declared that a Frémont ratification meeting at New York was designed to show that Frémont and McClellan were "twin cherries on one stem."[2] The *Boston Transcript* began to accuse Frémont of being in league with the Democrats,[3] and the *New York Times*, edited by Henry J. Raymond, who was Lincoln's campaign manager, took the same view.[4] The fact that the Democratic press devoted considerable space to the report of Frémont meetings gave enough color to the charge to make it hard to disprove.[5]

---

[1] June 29, 1864. [2] July 16, 1864.

[3] June 8, 11, 14, 1864.

[4] June 12, 1864; *National Republican*, June 14, 1864. "Petroleum V. Nasby," who had considerable vogue as a popular writer, used the argument that Frémont was in league with the Democrats, who in turn were in league with the Confederacy. See Locke, *The Moral History of America*, p. 123.

[5] The *Detroit Free Press*, July 29, 1864, declared that the contest in Michigan would be between Frémont and the Democrats.

Nevertheless, during June, July, and August the Frémont movement was an important factor in the political
situation, and some Republican journals, either by their
silence or by open statement, continued to oppose Lincoln.[6]
Frémont ratification meetings were held at many places. A
New York meeting was so well attended that the *New York
Times* felt called upon to explain that the meeting was large
because many Democrats were present.[7] At a great mass
meeting at Concord, where Frémont was supposed to deliver
an address, more than twenty thousand people gathered,
most of whom came for the sole purpose of hearing him
speak.[8] Wendell Phillips declared that he intended to con-
tinue his support of Frémont.[9] The *New York Tribune*
admitted that honest and conservative antislavery men who
were supporters of Frémont met at the Church of the Puri-
tan in New York to hear an address by Doctor Cheever, who
declared that the failure to support Frémont was the chief
mistake of the administration.[10] Enthusiastic Frémont meetings were held at Cincinnati, where it was claimed that Frémont was more popular than Lincoln,[11] and similar meetings
were held at other places in Ohio and in the Northwest.[12]
At a Frémont meeting in St. Louis, Congressman Henry T.
Blow and the mayor of the city were the important speakers,[13] and the Republican candidate for the governorship,
Colonel Fletcher, was a Frémont worker.[14] The *New York
Tribune* declared that the state of Missouri could not be carried for Lincoln if Frémont continued to be a candidate.[15]

The most important element in the support of Frémont
was the German population. The English traveler, Dicey,
who visited St. Louis, found that the Germans commanded

---

[6] See quotations in the *New Nation*, June 4, 1864.
[7] *New York Times*, June 28, 1864. The meeting was held June 27.
[8] *Liberator*, June 26, 1864.   [9] The *Crisis*, July 13, 1864.
[10] July 12, 1864; *Anti-Slavery Standard*, July 16, 1864.
[11] *Cincinnati Enquirer*, July 1, 1864.
[12] *Ohio Statesman*, July 16; *Ohio State Journal*, June 26; *Intelligencer*, June
29, 1864.
[13] *New Nation*, July 2, 1864.
[14] *New York Tribune*, August 4, 1864.
[15] *Ibid.*; also August 16, 1864.

the elections and were enthusiastic Frémont followers.[16] Reports came from that city that the Germans would stand for him through thick and thin.[17]   In Chicago where a German club, the "Arbeiter Verein" had a membership of 700 men, it was found that all but 103 favored the Frémont movement.[18]   It was declared that in Illinois in general the movement for him was quite formidable,[19] and it is probable that the German press of that state, for the most part, supported him.[20]   The *Cleveland Leader*, which was very anxious to find evidences of German support for Lincoln, could discover only five, or six German Lincoln journals.[21] Attempts were made also to establish new German papers for Frémont.[22]   *Der Demokrat* (Davenport, Iowa), declared that the majority of the Germans of Iowa supported Frémont, notwithstanding the fact that the administration press declared that there was no movement for him there.[23]   The local organizations of the society known as the "German National Club," were, as a general thing, centers of Frémont support.[24]

It is impossible to determine numerically the German support of Frémont, but some estimate may be made.   In 1860 the German population of Illinois was 130,891; that of New York State, 150,000; and the entire German population of the United States was 1,301,136.[25]   In Ohio, Indiana, Illinois, Missouri, and Pennsylvania, the Germans formed from 7 to 14 per cent of the population.[26]   Judging

---

[16] Dicey, *Six Months in the Federal States*, II, 167-68.

[17] *National Anti-Slavery Standard*, June 25, 1864.

[18] *Cleveland Leader*, May 29, and especially May 31, 1864.

[19] Flagg to Trumbull, June 24, 1864.   Trumbull MSS.

[20] *New York Tribune*, September 21, 1864.

[21] These were: *Abend Zeitung* (New York), *Staats Zeitung* (Illinois), *Wachter am Erie* (Cleveland), *Michigan Journal* (Detroit), *Volksblatt* (Cincinnati).   See *Cleveland Herald*, March 23, 1864.

[22] *Cincinnati Enquirer*, August 13, 1864.

[23] *Der Demokrat*, July 7, 1864.

[24] Koerner, *Memoirs*, II, 433.   On this subject see *Der Vestbote*, August 18, 1864. Of course some German papers were Democratic.   See Cole, *Era of the Civil War*, p. 322; also *Cincinnati Gazette*, July 13, 1864.

[25] *United States Census Report*, 1860, Introduction, pp. 28-30; *New York Times*, August 15, 1863.

[26] *Ibid.*

from the ardent support given to Frémont by such German journals as the *Neue Zeit*, St. Louis, and the *Pioneer* of Boston, and by the enthusiasm that seemed to prevail among them in general, it may be supposed that the great majority of the Germans would have voted for him. The effect that such a vote would have had on the election is mere speculation, but it is worth while to note that Lincoln's majority in New York State was only 6,749, and that the entire Lincoln majority throughout the country was only about 10 per cent of the voters.

In making an estimate of Frémont's strength, the abolitionists must be considered, although there is no way to evaluate their number. All that can be said is that he had a certain following among them.[27] Those who advocated General B. F. Butler for the presidency did so on the theory that Frémont had an important following and that he could be induced to withdraw in favor of Butler.[28] One writer may have stated the situation correctly when he said: "This Frémont movement is a weak concern, but just about as strong as the Birney movement which defeated Clay in 1844."[29]

It appears, therefore, that Frémont may have had a following of sufficient strength to defeat Lincoln, that is, by securing enough Republican votes to throw the election to the Democrats. The importance, then, of his candidacy, aside from its significance as a protest against the administration, depended on the closeness of the contest between the two major parties. For that reason, in appraising the importance of the Frémont movement, it is necessary to note the continued discontent among the Republicans in regard to the conduct of the administration.

Although Secretary Chase had withdrawn from the race for the Republican nomination and had remained in the Cabinet, he had done nothing to further the cause of his

---

[27] *National Anti-Slavery Standard*, July 16, 1864.
[28] E. Conkling to Butler, July 18, 1864; quoted in *B. F. Butler Correspondence*, IV, 512.
[29] Thomas B. Lincoln to Johnson, June 11, 1864. Johnson MSS.

chief, and it was patent that his relations with the President were not cordial.[30]   The continued friendship between the President and the Blairs, especially after Francis P. Blair, Jr., had bitterly attacked Chase,[31] together with what Chase thought was a curt note from the President in regard to the Pomeroy Circular,[32] did not make for more friendly relations between Lincoln and his Secretary of the Treasury.   Their relations came to a turning point over an appointment.

Late in June the assistant treasurer in New York City announced his desire to resign, and Chase wished to place one of the assistant secretaries of the Treasury, M. B. Field, in his place.   Senator Morgan of New York, however, desiring to control the patronage of his state, objected to the appointment of Field.[33]   Secretary Seward, who may have been interested in New York politics, and at any rate was not very friendly toward Chase, sided with Senator Morgan;[34] as a result, the President refused to appoint Field.[35]   Chase thought that the influence of the Blairs was at the bottom of the opposition to the appointment of his candidate, and he regarded the New York appointment as of sufficient importance to make an issue between himself and the President.[36] Chase had several times considered resigning from the Cabinet,[37] but for one reason or another had continued in office.[38]   He now sent in his resignation, and the President did not ask him to remain.[39]   The view taken by the Blairs in regard to this affair was stated by the elder Blair: "Chase,

[30] Adams, *Life of Dana*, II, 273-74.

[31] Blair attacked Chase in the House of Representatives April 23, 1864.

[32] Chase to Cooke, July 1, 1864; quoted in Oberholtzer, *Jay Cooke*, I, 421.

[33] Warden, *Chase*, p. 617; Schuckers, *Chase*, p. 484.

[34] Doster, *Lincoln and the Civil War*, p. 236; quotation from Doster's diary of June 30, 1864.

[35] Chittenden, *Recollections of Lincoln*, p. 379.

[36] Chase outlined his position to Jay Cooke, July 1, 1864.   See Oberholtzer, *Jay Cooke*, I, 421.

[37] In 1862, 1863, and 1864.   See Warden, *Chase*, p. 523; Riddle, *Recollections of War Times*, p. 275.

[38] Governor John Brough of Ohio was prominent among those who urged him to remain in the Cabinet.   See Brough to Chase, June 1, 1864, Chase MSS (Pa. Hist. Soc.).

[39] Fahnestock to Cooke, June 30, 1864; quoted in Oberholtzer, *Jay Cooke*, I, 420 and Warden, *Chase*, p. 614.

you see, hung on as long as possible and dropped at last like a rotten pear unexpectedly to himself [and] everybody else. He supposed he would bully Lincoln by threatening to resign unless he was permitted to make treasury appointments without control."[40] The formal break in the Cabinet could scarcely be regarded as anything but an indication that the President was not inclined to favor the more radical elements in the country, and it was particularly significant since the Baltimore convention had indicated its hostility to the Blair influence in the administration. About the time of the Chase withdrawal, Doster recorded in his diary that, of the New York journals, only the *Times* supported Lincoln with any force.[41]

The lack of Northern military success was another factor in the growing discontent with the President, a fact which the Frémont followers could make use of because they thought that Frémont should not have been removed from command. The appointment of General Grant to the commandership of the eastern forces had been hailed with approval by most Republicans, and for a time the enthusiasm for him had increased.[42] But as midsummer approached and he made no apparent progress against the Confederacy, there was a reaction. Senator Grimes reported from Washington that military critics regarded the campaign against Richmond as a failure,[43] and by the end of July his prestige had so declined that there was a general depression.[44] Some people in Pennsylvania and Maryland were even afraid of another Confederate invasion,[45] and the *New York Tribune* declared that, although it was reluctant to criticize, it was now willing to say that General Grant had failed in his campaign, and that the failure was due to blunders.[46]

---

[40] F. P. Blair to Frank [F. P. Blair, Jr.], July 4, 1864. Blair MSS.

[41] Doster, *Lincoln and the Civil War*, p. 236. This fact could be shown from the files of the journals; but Doster, who quotes from his diary, shows that it was recognized at the time.

[42] *New York Times*, December 31, 1863; Bloodgood to Chase, July 6, 1864. Chase MSS (Pa. Hist. Soc.).

[43] Grimes to Mrs. Grimes, June 19, 1864, quoted in Salter, *Grimes*, p. 263.

[44] Jay Cooke to Henry Cooke, August 2, 1864; quoted in Oberholtzer, *Jay Cooke*, I, 415.   [45] *Ibid.*   [46] August 5, 1864.

The suppression of the press by military authority was arousing a good deal of criticism against the administration. Although there had been some military suppression before 1864,[47] there was recurrence of it during the summer of that year. In July and August, the *Wheeling Register*, the *Parkersburg Gazette*, and the *Baltimore Bulletin* were suppressed by military order.[48] The Frémont faction had been particularly critical of the administration on the score of its interference with the freedom of the press, and now the *Daily Intelligencer* was added to the defenders of the press, declaring that Frémont was again the leader of "free soil, free speech, and Frémont," as he had been in 1856.[49]

More serious opposition to the President grew out of the problem of reconstruction. In December of 1863, the President had outlined his plan for reconstruction, which, however, was not drastic enough for many Republicans, and notably those very ones who were followers of Frémont. There were also others who had not taken any open stand for Frémont who were critical of the President on that point. In consequence, a measure less favorable to the South than the President's plan was framed, passed by both branches of Congress, and sent to the President on the last day of the session.[50] The President doubted the authority of Congress to act on the matter, and permitted the bill to fail by use of the pocket veto.[51] A few days later, July 8, he issued a proclamation concerning reconstruction, which amounted to a declaration that the President, not Congress, had control over that matter.[52]

Many Republicans were greatly incensed over the President's action. Prominent among these were Senators Sumner, Boutwell, Chandler, Wade, and Davis, and Congressmen Garfield, Schenck, and Whitmore.[53] Senator Wade, of

---

[47] *New York Tribune*, July 6, 1863; *New York Times*, July 12, 1863; *Crisis*, June 10, 1863.

[48] *Ohio Statesman*, July 15, 1864; *Daily Intelligencer*, July 20, 1864.

[49] *Daily Intelligencer*, August 9, September 2, 1864.

[50] 37th Cong., 2nd Sess., *Globe*, p. 3449; Pierce, *Sumner*, IV, 217.

[51] Nicolay and Hay, *Lincoln*, IX, 120-21.   [52] *Lincoln's Works*, II, 545.

[53] Warden, *Chase*, p. 625; Nicolay and Hay, *Lincoln*, IX, 121.

Ohio, and Senator Davis, of Maryland, drew up a protest against the President's action, which was published in the *New York Tribune,* August 5, 1864. The protest declared that the President's proclamation of July 8, was a "stupid outrage on the legislative authority of the people."[54] The criticism of the President by the Republican press was so common that the *New York Times,* the most prominent of the few political organs that consistently defended Lincoln, was frequently spoken of as an Administration rather than a Republican Journal.[55]

A Washington observer wrote that the Wade-Davis manifesto was like a bomb thrown into the city,[56] and Lincoln's friends spoke of Senator Wade and Senator Davis as public enemies comparable to the Confederates.[57] Chase learned that at Cincinnati the disaffection had grown to "abhorrence," and that every day the people were becoming more and more satisfied that "Honest Abe" was a "trixter."[58] The *Boston Transcript* declared that there was a great deal of uneasiness in the country,[59] and the *Ashtabula Sentinel,* which was influenced by Joshua Giddings but published in the home town of Senator Wade, found no fault with the manifesto, but made a mild statement against the idea of being critical of those in authority.[60]

The rising opposition to the President was shown by the political situation in Indiana. Schuyler Colfax, becoming convinced that drastic measures were needed to preserve the Republican power in that state, invented an ingenious scheme to accomplish that end. He proposed that General Sherman, with whom many Indiana regiments were located, should send home on leave of absence for the purpose of voting certain Republican soldiers, a list of whom Colfax would furnish. The scheme was proposed through Senator Sher-

---

[54] *New York Tribune,* August 5, 1864.
[55] *Daily Intelligencer,* August 15, 1864.
[56] Herbert to Butler, August 6, 1864; quoted in *B. F. Butler Correspondence,* V, 8.
[57] This is the statement of Montgomery Blair, *ibid.*
[58] Mellen to Chase, August 10, 1864. Chase MSS (Pa. Hist. Soc.).
[59] August 9, 1864.
[60] Quoted in *Ohio Statesman,* August 10, 1864.

man, who favored and advised the plan.[61] The General, however, was highly indignant, and declared that he could not spare the regiments; that it would be a breach of public law for him to use the army to interfere with civilian affairs; that his army was much more important than Congress; and that if the Republicans lost control of Congress, the new one could be no worse than the one then in power.[62] The scheme, therefore, was not carried out; but it shows how some politicians felt about the political situation, and how important a few Republican votes turned to Frémont might be.

Another insight into the political situation is furnished by the movement to make General B. F. Butler a compromise candidate for the presidency. It was represented to him that there was a growing impression throughout the North, and among Republicans, that a competent loyal man should be selected in place of President Lincoln, who was incompetent and surrounded by a Cabinet of like quality.[63] It was thought that Butler might be the man to take Lincoln's place, and the fact that it might be possible to get the "Frémont party" to support Butler was deemed of considerable importance.[64] This movement, like the earlier one for Grant, did not materialize.[65]

One of the most drastic contemporary statements concerning the political situation was made by Senator Sherman, of Ohio, who, outwardly at least, had taken no part in the movement against the President. The Senator declared that there was no enthusiasm for the political canvass, and that if the Democrats should select a candidate who had "any particle of patriotism or sense," they would sweep the Republicans out of office like an "avalanche." There was a general conviction, he said, that the President did not possess the "energy, dignity of character to either conduct the war or to

---

[61] Colfax to Senator John Sherman, August 2, 1864; and Senator John Sherman to General W. T. Sherman, August 6, 1864. W. T. Sherman MSS.

[62] W. T. Sherman to Senator John Sherman, August 12, 1864. W. T. Sherman MSS. Sherman was before Atlanta.

[63] Edgar Conkling to Butler, July 18, 1864; quoted in B. F. Butler Correspondence, IV, 510.   [64] Ibid.

[65] This was the movement for him at the Cleveland Convention.

make peace."[66] About the same time Thurlow Weed declared that Lincoln could not possibly be elected, and that unless a hundred thousand men could be raised soon, the Union cause would be lost.[67] Lincoln was reported to have said: "You think I don't know I am going to be beaten, but I do, and unless some great change takes place beaten badly."[68]

Carl Schurz ably summarized the points of criticism that were being formed against Lincoln as follows: the lack of success in military enterprises; the opposition to his schemes for reconstruction; his conduct of public business; and his lack of energy in carrying on the war.[69] The importance, therefore, of the Frémont movement and the Republican votes which he might receive was accentuated by the opposition to the President. This, aside from the general disapproval of the Democrats, was represented by the Chase-Pomeroy group, the Wade-Davis group, the Butler group, and by the general dissatisfaction as represented by Senator Sherman—all of which might work to the advantage of Frémont.

In view of the situation, therefore, it seemed for a time that Frémont might be able to force the President out of the race, for a movement was started to secure the withdrawal of both Lincoln and Frémont, and the selection of a new candidate. Talk of such an idea was rumored about during the latter part of July, and the President, hearing of it, expressed the doubt that there was anyone who could secure more support than he.[70] But, as the month of August advanced, the desire to have him out of the way increased. Mrs. B. F. Butler, writing from Lowell, Massachusetts, stated that Lincoln's chances for re-election were less and less every day and that unless he and Frémont should withdraw and a new candidate be selected, the Democrats would

---

[66] Senator John Sherman to General W. T. Sherman, July 24, 1864. W. T. Sherman MSS.

[67] Herbert to Butler, August 6, 1864; quoted in *B. F. Butler Correspondence*, V, 9.

[68] Herbert to Butler, August 11, 1864; quoted in *Ibid.*, p. 35.

[69] Schurz, *Reminiscences*, III, 98-99.

[70] *Ibid.*, p. 100.

win the election.[71] Butler's friends in New York informed
him that practically all of the public men of that city de-
spaired of Lincoln's election and believed that a new Republican convention should be held after the meeting of the
Democratic convention on September 1, 1864.[72] This idea
was fast taking form and resulted in a meeting held at New
York, August 18, at which a decision was made to send a
circular letter to certain prominent men, asking their opinions
on the question of a new convention, and to hold a second
meeting, August 30, at the home of David Dudley Field to
consider the replies.[73] Prominent among the leaders in this
movement, besides David Dudley Field, were Charles Sumner, Governor Andrew (Mass.), Thurlow Weed (N. Y.),
Leonard Sweet (Maine), George Wilkes (Editor of *Wilkes
Spirit of the Times*, N. Y.), and Senator Wade (Ohio).[74]
Hume, who attended the meeting, said that twenty-five
prominent men were present.[75]

---

[71] Mrs. Butler to B. F. Butler, August 13, 1864; quoted in *B. F. Butler Correspondence*, V, 47.

[72] Shaffer to B. F. Butler, August 17, 1864; quoted *ibid.*, p. 67.

[73] Pearson, *Life of Andrew*, II, 159-60.

[74] *Ibid.*; Colonel Shaffer to Butler, August 17, 1864; quoted in *B. F. Butler Correspondence*, V, 67.

[75] Hume, *Abolitionists*, 178-79.

CHAPTER X

THE WITHDRAWAL OF FRÉMONT

The candidacy of General Frémont seemed a definite obstacle to the realignment of forces which were preparing for a vigorous struggle against the Democratic opposition, and a separate movement was started to secure his withdrawal. About August 20, several prominent abolitionists, including Eleaseur Wright and G. L. Stearns, wrote to Frémont in regard to the matter.[1] Frémont replied that in consideration of his nomination by the Cleveland convention, he did not feel at liberty to withdraw without consulting the party that had nominated him, but that at any rate the existing arrangement should not be changed unless arrangements were made for a new nomination; he suggested that he would be willing to submit the whole question to a new convention.[2] He did not say that he would not be a candidate before that convention, and he may have thought that he had an even chance of being the new nominee. Frémont also suggested three propositions on the basis of which a new convention should be assembled: a guaranty that the practical liberty and constitutional rights and dignity of the people should be respected; the maintenance of the dignity of the United States in their relation to foreign powers; and the re-establishment of the Union by peace of possible, by war if necessary. He explained that the abolition of slavery should be a requisite of peace, but intimated that it might be compensated abolition.

The movement for a new convention, however, depended on the outcome of the project started at New York. Various

---

[1] *Ohio State Journal*, August 27, 1864, gives Frémont's reply; the *Crisis*, September 4, 1864, printed the letters.
[2] *Ibid.*

replies were received to the letters sent out by the New York committee. Senator Henry Winter Davis, of Maryland, favored the movement and urged that as many men as possible should be assembled at the next meeting, August 30.[3] John Jay suggested that a letter might be prepared and sent to Lincoln, which would either force him to withdraw or to promise a more drastic antislavery policy, as the price of their support.[4] A promise of a more radical antislavery policy would, of course, be an admission that Frémont had been correct in his policies all along. General B. F. Butler favored the idea and suggested Fisher A. Hildreth or N. G. Upham as men who could explain his opinions.[5] Lucius Robinson was enthusiastic and mentioned General Grant or General Dix as compromise candidates.[6]

From the office of the *Cincinnati Gazette* came a very hearty response. Richard Smith of that journal believed that the Republicans would fail unless such a measure was carried out. "The people," he said, "regard Mr. Lincoln's candidacy as a misfortune. His apparent strength when nominated was fictitious, and now fiction has disappeared and instead of confidence there is disgust. I do not know a Lincoln man in all our correspondence, which is large and varied, and I have seen few letters from Lincoln men."[7] Horace Greeley declared that "Lincoln is already beaten. He cannot be elected and we must have another ticket to save us from utter overthrow."[8] He suggested Grant, Butler, or General Sherman. Chase was evasive. He said that previous engagements prevented him from attending the meeting on August 30, and at any rate he was not sure as to how he stood on the matter.[9] Senator Henry Winter Davis was one of the most active workers for the new convention. He requested Clement B. Barclay to present the project to various promi-

---

[3] Davis to [Field], August 26, 1864; quoted in *New York Sun*, June 30, 1889.
[4] Jay to [Field], August 29, 1864; *ibid.*
[5] Butler to [Field], August 29, 1864; *ibid.*
[6] Robinson to [Field], August 29, 1864; *ibid.*
[7] Smith to [Field], August 27, 1864; *ibid.*
[8] Greeley to Opdyke, August 18, 1864; *ibid.*
[9] Chase to Opdyke, August 18, 1864; *ibid.*

nent men of Philadelphia, and asked that Secretary of War Cameron be approached. He believed that Maryland, the New England States, Pennsylvania, Delaware, Ohio, and Michigan would favor the new convention.[10] Senator Sumner agreed with Davis in regard to the situation in New England.[11]

There were a few dissenting voices. Senator Wade, of Ohio, although agreeing with the radical faction in most matters, was afraid that there might be action without due preparation, and advised further deliberation.[12] Roscoe Conkling refused to take part in the affair, yet he declared that the Republicans were slipping "down stream with a rapidity" which would make a landing whether they paddled or not.[13] J. S. Prettyman, of Delaware, admitted that the rank and file of the Republicans were dissatisfied with President Lincoln, but he thought that they were afraid to say so for fear of aiding the Democrats. He thought that it would be all right if a new convention could force Lincoln out; but, if it could not, then it would only bring further confusion.[14] J. Collamer directly refused to aid in the movement because he thought the party should stand by its nominee however poor his chances for success might appear to be.[15]

The proposed meeting took place as arranged on August 30, 1864. It was decided that Horace Greeley, Park Goodwin of the *New York Evening Post,* and Theodore Tilton of the *New York Independent* should write a joint letter to the Republican governors of the Northern states and ask them three questions: whether or not Lincoln's election were a probability; whether he could carry their respective states; and whether they thought that the interest of the Republican party and of the country demanded another candidate who would inspire more confidence than did Lincoln.[16]

---

[10] Davis to Opdyke, August 25, 1864; *ibid.*
[11] Pearson, *Life of Andrew,* II, 160, quotation from Sumner.
[12] Davis to Opdyke, August 25, 1864; quoted in *New York Sun,* June 30, 1889.
[13] Conkling to [Field], August 28, 1864; *ibid.*
[14] Prettyman to [Field], August 30, 1864; *ibid.*
[15] Collamer to J. A. Stevens, August 25, 1864; *ibid.*
[16] Pearson, *Life of Andrew,* II, 161-62.

Frémont had made known his position in regard to a new convention; but President Lincoln, although he was well informed as to the situation, had made no commitment. About the middle of August, Thurlow Weed told him that his re-election was an impossibility,[17] and at a meeting of the Republican National Executive Committee, about August 22, it was decided that Henry J. Raymond, chairman of the Committee and editor of the *New York Times*, should write to Lincoln in regard to the situation.[18] Raymond, therefore, informed him that according to the indications, Illinois, Pennsylvania, Indiana, and New York were likely to be against him, and suggested that the war might be brought to an end if the idea of abolition were abandoned and that fact definitely published.[19]

In the meantime the Democratic convention met at Chicago. Republican journals had pointed out that Frémont would like to have the Democratic nomination, and the fact that Caspar Butz was present at the Chicago convention advocating Frémont's nomination lends color to the charge.[20] There had been, however, a movement of more than two years standing favoring General McClellan,[21] and his selection came as the result of positive Democratic sentiment.[22]

The agitation against President Lincoln continued. Francis Lieber declared that in times of revolution popularity wore out quickly and that Lincoln's case was no exception. He wished, he said, that an "angel could descend and show him (Lincoln) what a beautiful stamp on his name in history" would be produced by his voluntary withdrawal.[23] One of Frémont's followers, Emil Pretorius, favored a new convention, and promised to confer with the Frémont committee in St. Louis to see what sort of a scheme could be

---

[17] Nicolay and Hay, *Lincoln*, IX, 250.   [18] *Ibid.*, p. 218.
[19] *Ibid.* Lincoln arrived at the conclusion about August 22 that he could not be re-elected.
[20] *National Anti-Slavery Standard*, September 17, 1864.
[21] Buchanan to Coryell, September 6, 1864, Coryell MSS; Barnes, *Weed Memoirs*, p. 428; Jay to Chase, October 2, 1864. Chase MSS.
[22] *New York Tribune*, February 23, 1864.
[23] Lieber to Gen. Halleck, September 1, 1864; quoted in Perry, *Lieber*, p. 350.

devised.[24] In Illinois, where Frémont had a strong following and where McClellan's candidacy was popular, there was ready support for a new nomination.[25] Governor Andrew, of Massachusetts, Senator Sumner, Whitelaw Reid, and others continued to promote the project for a new convention, and on September 3 it was arranged for Senator Chandler to visit Lincoln and demand that he should immediately dismiss several of his Cabinet members. It was thought that such a move would bring matters to a show-down on the part of Lincoln.[26]

Two events, however, were in the making which changed the whole political situation. One was the fact that General McClellan was proving to be a popular candidate,[27] which tended to cause the Republicans to pass over their own difficulties, and the second was the capture of Atlanta by General Sherman, the news of which reached the North on the same day that it was decided that Senator Chandler should make his demands of the President. Senator Sherman declared that, although Lincoln lacked dignity, energy, and business capacity, yet in face of the united Democratic support of McClellan, it was necessary to support him. It would become, therefore, even more essential to conciliate the Frémont group. Senator Henry Winter Davis became anxious, declaring that the call for the new convention should be made before it was too late;[28] but C. B. Sedgwick believed that the time had already passed, since the Atlanta victory would cause Lincoln to refuse to withdraw.[29]

For the moment those who favored a new convention did not know exactly what to do. Leonard Sweet, arriving in New York on September 8, found Greeley, Beecher, Ray-

---

[24] E. Pretorius to [Field], September 1, 1864; quoted in *New York Sun*, June 30, 1889.

[25] Martin to Trumbull, September 2, 1864. Trumbull MSS.

[26] Sumner to [Field], September 1, 1864, and Reid to [Field], September 2, 1864, quoted in *New York Sun*, June 30, 1889; Pearson, *Life of Andrew*, II, 106; Herbert to Butler, September 3, 1864, quoted in *B. F. Butler Correspondence*, V, 120.

[27] Senator Sherman to W. T. Sherman, September 4, 1864, Sherman MSS; Henry Winter Davis to [Field], September 4, 1864, quoted in *New York Sun*, June 30, 1889.

[28] Davis to [Field], September 4, 1864; quoted in *New York Sun*, June 30, 1889.

[29] Sedgwick to [Field], September 7, 1864; *ibid.*

mond, and Weed greatly depressed, and still talking about a new convention.[30] On September 5, W. C. Bryant, of the *Evening Post*, declared that he was "so disgusted with Lincoln's behavior that he could not muster enough courage to write to him";[31] and on the twelfth Governor Morton of Indiana was so concerned over the situation in his state that he was afraid soldiers would be needed to preserve order in case the draft was continued, and asked Secretary of War Stanton to send 15,000 soldiers there to vote in the election.[32]

The fall of Atlanta seems to have been the determining factor in the situation. Sedgwick declared that it had turned the tide.[33] "The fall of Atlanta," said one writer, "puts an entirely new aspect upon the face of affairs. The McClellan party is in check—God be praised."[34] By September 12, the idea of a new convention was abandoned.[35] The *New York Tribune* declared that there had been a great deal of dissatisfaction with the military campaign, and that if the Republican nominating convention had been held in September, another leader might have been chosen; but now it had become evident that it was necessary to choose between Lincoln and McClellan, and that the *Tribune* would fly the Lincoln banner.[36] In general the political leaders took a new interest and began a new effort to unite the party.[37] In that case, obviously, both Chase and Frémont had to be conciliated.

President Lincoln had not remained inactive; his efforts are clearly seen in his conduct towards Chase. Chief Justice Taney had been in very ill health for some time, his death being expected at any moment, and Chase was ambitious for his place. Chase, therefore, began to bring whatever influence

---

[30] Sweet to his wife, September 8, 1864; quoted in Tarbell, *Life of Lincoln*, II, 202.

[31] Bryant to Forbes, September 5, 1864; quoted in Hughes, *Forbes*, II, 101.

[32] Merton to Stanton, September 12, 1864. Stanton MSS.

[33] Sedgwick to Forbes, September 5, 1864; quoted in Hughes, *Forbes*, II, 101.

[34] Henry Elliott to Welles, September 5, 1864. Welles, MSS.

[35] Geo. Wilkes to Butler, September 15, 1864, quoted in *B. F. Butler Correspondence*, V, 134; Williams to Stevens, September 15, 1864, quoted in *New York Sun*, June 30, 1889.

[36] *New York Tribune*, September 6, 1864.

[37] Pearson, *Life of Andrew*, II, 164.

he could upon Lincoln to secure a promise of the appointment to the supreme bench whenever the vacancy occurred. He enlisted the aid of such men as Schuyler Colfax, who wrote to the President, pointing out that Chase had "not unimportant judicial talent," and that he was "sound on the great financial, military, and political questions" that would arise.[38] What commitments President Lincoln made are not exactly known, but Senator Morgan later affirmed that Lincoln told him that he had promised Chase the chief justiceship in order to gain his support.[39] Whitelaw Reid declared to Chase: "Either Mr. Lincoln has determined to make you Chief Justice or he has determined to make your friends believe so until after the election."[40] Greeley believed that the President had committed himself,[41] and a Washington observer noted that the President had sent for Chase, who, after a long interview, had agreed to go to Ohio in order to aid in the campaign, and the belief in Washington was that the judicial post was the bargain.[42] In all probability, therefore, Chase was given a definite promise, and it seems reasonable, for that situation explains the attitude of Chase toward the new convention which had for an object the displacement of Lincoln. At any rate he came out boldly for Lincoln on September 19, and in December he was appointed to the chief-justiceship.[43]

The President continued to work in his own behalf. After the fall of Atlanta he asked General Logan to leave the Army for a time and to assist in the campaign, especially in Illinois, where the Republican defection was thought to be strong.[44] He arranged for Carl Schurz to leave the Army in

[38] Colfax to Chase, October 24, 1864. Chase MSS (Pa. Hist. Soc.).

[39] Morgan told this to Bigelow in 1867. Morgan quoted from his diary of April 3, 1865; quoted in Bigelow, *Retrospections*, IV, 57.

[40] Reed to Chase, October 19, 1864. Chase MSS (Pa. Hist. Soc.).

[41] Chase to Greeley, October 21, 1864. Chase MSS (New York Pub. Lib.).

[42] Herbert to Butler, September 26, 1864; quoted in *B. F. Butler Correspondence*, V, 167.

[43] The fact that he spoke to a visiting delegation in favor of Lincoln on September 19, is recorded in the *New Nation*, September 24, 1864. For his appointment see *Crisis*, December 14, 1864.

[44] For this whole story see Mrs. Logan's *Reminiscences*, p. 167. General Sherman said he remembered receiving a telegram asking for Logan's services.

order to make speeches,[45] and there were other examples of both officers and men who were furloughed for political reasons.[46] He secured the support of Weed by the removal of Hiram Barney from the customs house in New York,[47] and in turn Weed acted as the President's envoy in getting the support of the *New York Herald,* the editor of which later was offered the ambassadorship at Paris.[48] The support of the *Evening Post* was secured through the efforts of John W. Forbes.[49]

It seems, therefore, that the Republican ranks were being rapidly closed save for the Frémont breach. It was clear that Frémont could have no basis for hope that his position would be of more importance than a diverting factor within the Republican ranks. Some journals and individuals were attempting to show that the movement for him was entirely dead.[50] But it appears that he had about the same strength that he possessed earlier in the year. Frémont meetings continued to be held; radical Republican, abolitionist, and German support continued.[51] An important consideration is the President's opinion in regard to the importance of Frémont's following. Fortunately his view has been preserved. He thought that the German voters who would support Frémont were of sufficient numbers to turn the election in New York, Wisconsin, and Illinois against him.[52]

In consideration that Frémont had indicated a willingness to withdraw in case of a new convention, several politicians began to seek a way to accomplish that and still leave Lincoln in the race. They hit upon the idea of having Montgomery Blair removed from the Cabinet as an indication

---

[45] Schurz, *Reminiscences,* III, 101, 108, 110.

[46] Tarbell, *Lincoln,* III, 203, 204.

[47] This is Senator Morgan's story. See Bigelow, *Retrospection,* IV, 57.

[48] Weed, *Autobiography,* p. 616.

[49] Pearson, *Life of Andrew,* II, 164.

[50] *Boston Transcript,* August 26, 1864; *New Nation,* October 1, 1864; *New York Times,* July 27, 1864; Conkling to Trumbull, June 29, 1864, Trumbull MSS; Mansfield to Chase, August 25, 1864, Chase MSS.

[51] *Cincinnati Gazette,* August 17, 1864; *Crisis,* August 10, 1864; *National Anti-Slavery Standard,* October 8, 1864; *New Nation,* August 27, 1864.

[52] Koerner, *Memoirs,* II, 432. Koerner talked with Lincoln about this time and reports what the President said.

that the President was willing to make some concession to the Frémont forces.

It is more or less of a mystery why Montgomery Blair was appointed to the Cabinet, but apparently he was the personal choice of the President.[53] From the first, many cabinet discussions hinged about the Blairs, and especially in controversies involving Chase and Frémont. The open hostility between Frémont and the Blairs had continued since 1861; Chase had felt that he could not remain in the Cabinet when their influence on the President was uppermost; and the national convention had hinted that Lincoln should rid himself of their influence. "We are on the brink of a fearful precipice . . . ," declared Garfield in 1864. "The President is bound hand and foot by the Blairs and they are dragging him and the country down into the chasm."[54] Thurlow Weed was opposed to them,[55] and Gideon Welles was informed that the "dislike of the Blairs amounts to positive hatred."[56] When Lincoln appointed Francis P. Blair, Jr., to an army command after his attack on Chase in the House, it was reported from Cincinnati that the President had done nothing which excited so much indignation since his revocation of Frémont's emancipation order.[57]

The scheme was developed, therefore, to play Frémont against the Blairs, and Senator Chandler of Michigan was the leader in this plan.[58] He determined not only to remove the Blair difficulty and secure the support or withdrawal of Frémont, but also to gain the co-operation of the Wade-Davis group, all at one stroke. Chandler visited Wade, who agreed that if the President would show enough deference to public opinion to remove some of the more obnoxious members of his Cabinet, he would be more friendly to his re-election; and at any rate Wade said that he would agree to do whatever his friend Senator Henry Winter Davis

[53] See account in Weed's *Autobiography*, p. 607.
[54] Smith, *Garfield*, I, 377.
[55] *National Anti-Slavery Standard*, October 8, 1864.
[56] James Boles to Welles, April 27, 1864. Welles MSS.
[57] Heaton to Chase, April 29, 1864. Chase MSS (Pa. Hist. Soc.).
[58] This was about August 8, 1864.

would do.[59] Chandler then visited Lincoln and received his promise that Blair would be removed if that would cause harmony in the party, and Senator Davis agreed that such an act would be a manifestation of the good intentions of the President. Chandler then went to New York and opened negotiations with the Frémont leaders. David Jerome (Mich.), E. O. Grosvenor (Ohio), George Wilkes (N. Y.), and Senator Chandler held conferences at the Astor House over a three- or four-day period, and the agreement was made that Frémont was to withdraw, with the understanding that Blair was to be removed.[60] Others had been at work on independent movements to secure a Blair-Frémont arrangement. Judge Ebenezer Peck of Illinois had secured a promise from Lincoln to remove Blair if that act would close the Frémont breach,[61] and Horace Greeley apparently promised Frémont that both Stanton and Blair would be removed.[62]

Frémont carried out his part of the agreement, announcing on September 22 that he was no longer to be considered as a candidate.[63] He declared that the union of the Republican party was paramount, since the Democrats stood for reestablishment of the Union with slavery. Yet he could not depart from the arena without one parting fling at the President. "I consider," he said, "that his administration has been politically, militarily, and financially a failure and that its necessary continuance is a cause of regret to the country."[64] On September 23, the President addressed a polite note to Montgomery Blair, asking him to resign. The latter promptly turned in his resignation,[65] and Senator Chandler, who felt that the whole negotiation was a personal success, held a "celebration," in honor of the event.[66]

---

[59] The whole story of Chandler's part in the affair is told in the *Post-Tribune Life of Chandler*, pp. 273-76.
[60] *Ibid.*   [61] Laughlin, *Missouri Politics*, p. 147.
[62] Sawyer to Frémont, September 3, 1864. Andrew Johnson MSS.
[63] The notice was dated September 19, but appeared in various journals September 22, 1864.   [64] *Ibid.*
[65] Both notes were quoted in various journals. They can be found in the *Crisis*, September 28, 1864.
[66] Herbert to Butler, September 26, 1864; quoted in *B. F. Butler Correspondence*, V, 167.

Frémont understood that the President would make other removals besides that of Blair,[67] but when Lincoln told the story of the affair to Senator Morgan he mentioned the promise to remove the Postmaster-General, but no one else.[68] The belief was current, however, that Lincoln, if elected, had agreed to select a new Cabinet at the beginning of his second term.[69] The removal of Blair did not cause much of a stir at Washington, for there was apparently little regret among the majority of the politicians to see him out of the Cabinet.[70] In a New York speech Blair explained his resignation by saying that his father advised the move.[71] He continued, however, to be on friendly terms with the President.[72]

After Frémont's withdrawal, he presided over a Republican meeting in New York to show that he had come to the support of the party,[73] but the Frémont organ, the *New Nation*, did not immediately abandon the idea of a separate candidate, and issued a belated call for a new nomination.[74] The *Neue Zeit* declared that although Frémont had abandoned them, they still hoped to have a candidate to oppose Lincoln,[75] and the St. Louis *Westliche Post* advised its readers to refrain from voting as a protest to the whole political situation.[76]

It is difficult to be precise about the influence of Frémont's withdrawal on the outcome of the election. The *Cleveland Leader* believed that thousands of Germans would thereby be brought into the Lincoln camp.[77] It was thought that his withdrawal caused a considerable element in Michigan to come to the support of Lincoln, and the Republican defection in Michigan was important.[78] Gradually many

[67] Sawyer to Frémont, September 13, 1865. Andrew Johnson MSS (copy).
[68] See Bigelow, *Retrospections*, IV, 57.
[69] Shaffer to Butler; quoted in *B. F. Butler Correspondence*, IV, 57.
[70] Doster, *Lincoln and the Civil War*, p. 175. See Welles to Mrs. Welles, September 23, 1864, Welles MSS, for another view.
[71] *Ohio Statesman*, October 3, 1864.
[72] The President continued to advise with Blair.
[73] Riddle, *Recollections*, p. 294.   [74] *New Nation*, September 17, 1864.
[75] Quoted in *National Anti-Slavery Standard*, October 1, 1864.
[76] *Westliche Post*, quoted in *Crisis*, November 16, 1864.
[77] *Cleveland Leader*, September 24, 1864.
[78] Dilla, *Politics of Michigan*, p. 36.

German journals such as the *Missouri Radikale,* which had
been founded as a Frémont organ, and the *Chicago Telegraph* came out for Lincoln.[79] Although some of the German press went over to the Democrats, it was thought that
for the most part the Germans supported Lincoln.[80] When
the election was over the *Chicago Tribune* believed that the
German voters had greatly aided the Republican cause.[81]

One of Frémont's friends believed that the "Radical
Democracy," as Frémont's party was called, accomplished
three definite results: it caused the Republicans to model
their platform after that of the Cleveland convention; it
caused the removal from the Cabinet of the element most
hostile to the ideas of the radicals; and it caused the President to assume a more drastic stand against slavery.[82]

---

[79] *New York Tribune,* September 29, October 2, 1864.
[80] *New Nation,* October 15, 1864.
[81] See Cole, *Era of the Civil War,* p. 328.
[82] *Daily Intelligencer,* October 18, 1864.

CHAPTER XI

CRITICAL ESSAY ON AUTHORITIES

Historical literature dealing with the general subject of the Civil War is of tremendous volume. Practically all libraries of importance have collections of documents, unpublished manuscripts, and personal reminiscences, but as yet there is no adequate guide to this maze of history. The best general biography of John C. Frémont is, *Frémont: the West's Greatest Adventurer* (2 vols., N. Y., 1928), written by Allan Nevins. For the purpose of political use during the campaign of 1856, several biographies of Frémont appeared, dealing largely with his explorations and based on his official reports. The chapters covering his early life in John Bigelow's *Life and Public Service of John Charles Frémont* (N. Y., 1856) were written by Mrs. Frémont. Late in life, faced with economic need, and encouraged by the success which followed the publication of Grant's *Memoirs,* Frémont published the first volume of *Memoirs of My Life* (N. Y., 1886), but the failure of this effort to meet with financial success prevented the publication of the second volume, which would have dealt with his career after 1856. The best bibliography of Frémont's explorations is found in Frederick S. Dellenbaugh's *Frémont and '49* (N. Y., 1914).

H. H. Bancroft's *History of California* (6 vols., San Francisco, 1888) discusses Frémont's senatorial career, but with lack of critical analysis. Very valuable data can be found in R. G. Cleland's *A History of California* (N. Y., 1922), and Z. S. Elridge's *History of California* (5 vols., N. Y., 1915). One should also consult *The Beginnings of San Francisco* (2 vols., San Francisco, 1912), by the same author, and Cardinal Goodwin's *The Establishment of State*

Government in California (N. Y., 1914). Thomas H. Benton's *Thirty Years View*, is valuable.

The most important materials for the early political phases of Frémont's life are found in the newspapers of California, particularly the *Daily Alta California* (San Francisco), *California Courier*, the *San José Argus* and the *Daily Pacific News*. The letters and news items from California, printed in the *New York Tribune*, are valuable.

The various collections of Salmon P. Chase MSS are indispensable for the student studying the decade preceding the War, as well as the War period itself. The main collection is in the Library of Congress, but the Pennsylvania Historical Society Library possesses about twenty-eight boxes of letters, containing some of the originals of the copies found in the former collection. There are Chase MSS in the New York Public Library and collections elsewhere. For the Fillmore movement of 1856, one should consult the John Bell MSS, and the John J. Crittenden MSS. The John McLean MSS shed considerable light upon McLean's candidacy in 1856. The William Schouler MSS give useful data on some of the inner workings of Congress during the strife over the speakership in 1856; Schouler had a large and varied correspondence. The Gideon Welles MSS are useful for the year of 1856, as well as for later times, and the student should consult the Levi Lincoln MSS, the W. P. Mangum MSS, the W. P. Fessenden MSS, the Thomas Ewing MSS, the William L. Marcey MSS, and the John Bigelow MSS.

The materials for a study of the movement that resulted in Frémont's nominations are very scattered. One should not overlook James S. Pike's *First Blows of the Civil War* (N. Y., 1879), which contains letters, newspaper quotations, and other valuable material. John McLean's letters are found in William Salter (ed.), *Letters of John McLean to John Teasdale* (Cincinnati, 1899). The *Life and Times of Samuel Bowles* (2 vols., N. Y., 1885), by George S. Merriam, is of special value. Bowles was editor of the *Springfield* (Mass.) *Republican* and had a wide correspondence.

Materials concerning the movement for Chase are to be found in William Salter's *Life of James W. Grimes* (N. Y., 1876). Grimes was governor of Iowa and later a senator. The two biographies of Chase, one by James W. Schuckers, *Life and Public Service of Salmon P. Chase* (N. Y., 1874), and the other by Robert B. Warden, bearing the same title (Cincinnati, 1874), should be examined. The interest of Seward in the nomination can be traced in Frederick Seward's *Seward at Washington as Senator and Secretary of State* (5 vols., N. Y., 1891), and in *Memoirs of Thurlow Weed* (Boston, 1884), by T. W. Barnes, who was Weed's grandson.

For a study of the activity of the German citizens in the campaign, probably Frederic Bancroft's collection of the *Speeches, Correspondence, and Papers of Carl Schurz* (6 vols., N. Y., 1908) is the most valuable. This should be checked, however, with the *Memoirs of Gustave Koerner*, edited by Thomas J. McCormack (2 vols., Cedar Rapids, 1909), and the *Reminiscences of Carl Schurz* (3 vols., N. Y., 1913). Some of the most important German journals were: *Der Demokrat* (Davenport, Iowa), *Der Westbote* (Columbus, Ohio), *Volksfreund* and *Wachter am Erie* (both of Cleveland, Ohio), and the *Boston Pioneer*. A brief biography of Frémont made its appearance in New York during the campaign.

The compilation of the *Correspondence of Robert Toombs, Alexander H. Stevens, and Howell Cobb,* by U. B. Phillips (A. H. R., 1911, Vol. II), is very valuable for Southern opinion; and Arthur C. Cole's *The Whig Party in the South* (Washington, 1913) is valuable. In general, however, one has to turn to Southern newspapers for information. The *Richmond Enquirer*, the *Louisiana Courier*, the *Augusta Constitutionalist*, and the *Daily Union* (Washington) are good sources for the Democratic slant on the events of the time. The Fillmore point of view can perhaps best be found in the *Baltimore American* and the *Nashville Whig*.

Indiana politics for the period are well covered by Charles Zimmerman, "Origin and Rise of the Republican Party in Indiana," *Indiana Magazine of History* (Vol. XIII, 1917); in Frémont C. Brand, "The History of the Know-Nothing Party in Indiana," *Indiana Magazine of History* (Vol. XVIII, 1922); and in Logan Esarey, *History of Indiana* (3 vols., Indianapolis, 1913). The same service for the state of Illinois has been rendered by Arthur C. Cole in his *Era of the Civil War* (Vol. III of the *Centennial History of Illinois*, Springfield, 1919). The work by Albert J. Beveridge, *Abraham Lincoln: 1809-1858* (Boston, 1928) is of considerable value. The Political situation in Michigan is treated in Hariette M. Dilla's *The Politics of Michigan* (Washington, 1904) and in Floyd B. Streeter's *Political Parties in Michigan* (Lansing, 1908). The study by Carlyle Buley, "The Political Balance in the Old Northwest, 1820-1865," in *Studies in American History Inscribed to Albert J. Woodburn* (Bloomington, Indiana, 1926) is good; and the compilation of the *Detroit Post and Tribune, An Outline Sketch of the Life and Public Service of Zachariah Chandler* (Detroit, 1880), is valuable but not critical. One of the best works dealing with Missouri politics is S. B. Laughlin's *Missouri Politics during the Civil War* (Iowa City, 1921). The most valuable work for New Jersey is Charles M. Knapp's *New Jersey Politics During the Civil War and Reconstruction* (Geneva, N. Y., 1924); and Lewis Pelzer's "The Origin of the Republican Party in Iowa," in the *Iowa Journal of History and Politics* (Vol. IV, 1906) is the best account of the rise of the Republican party in Iowa.

The most valuable single collection of source material for the study of the Civil War is the *War of the Rebellion: The Official Record of the Union and Confederate Armies* (Washington, 1880-1901). Almost equally important for the study of the Frémont episode in Missouri is Volume III of the *Report of the Joint Committee on the Conduct of the War, Senate Reports, 37th Cong., 3d Sess.*, No. 108. The *Report of the Committee on Government Contracts, House*

Report, 37th Cong., 2d Sess., No. 1, should be examined. John H. Howard's *Reminiscences of Things Past* (N. Y., 1925) is an account written by one of Frémont's staff. A good résumé of the Missouri situation in 1861 is E. C. Smith, *The Borderland in the Civil War* (N. Y., 1927).

One of the best studies of the Radical Republican movement in 1864 is Arthur C. Cole's "President Lincoln and the Illinois Radical Republicans," *Mississippi Valley Historical Review,* Vol. IV, 1918. The John A. Andrew MSS shed some light on the subject, Andrew being a friend both of Frémont and of the Blairs. The Chase MSS are indispensable, and the John Sherman MSS disclose some of the ideas concerning Lincoln that were held by some of his most staunch supporters. John Bigelow's *Retrospections of an Active Life* (5 Vols., N. Y., 1909) is of special value. The Gideon Welles MSS and the *Diary of Gideon Welles* (3 vols., Boston, 1911) contain material of importance, although the *Diary* was somewhat revised in later years. The *New York Sun* for June 30, 1889, printed a very valuable collection of letters bearing on the movement to force President Lincoln to withdraw from the presidential race in 1864.

INDEX